CAMBRIDGE MUSIC H*

Dowland: *Lachrimae* (1604)

Dowland's *Lachrimae* (1604) is perhaps the greatest but most enigmatic publication of instrumental music from before the eighteenth century. This new handbook, the first detailed study of the collection, investigates its publication history, its instrumentation, its place in the history of Renaissance dance music, and its reception history. Two extended chapters examine the twenty-one pieces in the collection in detail, discussing the complex internal relationships between the cycle of seven 'Lachrimae' pavans, the relationships between them and other pieces inside and outside the collection, and possible connections between the Latin titles of the seven pavans and Elizabethan conceptions of melancholy. The extraordinarily multi-faceted nature of the collection also leads the author to illuminate questions of patronage, the ordering and format of the collection, pitch and transposition, tonality and modality, and even numerology.

PETER HOLMAN is director of The Parley of Instruments, the choir Psalmody and the vocal ensemble Seicento, as well as musical director of Opera Restor'd. He has recently been appointed Reader in Musicology at Leeds University, and is the author of *Four and Twenty Fiddlers: the Violin at the English Court 1540–1690* and *Henry Purcell.*

CAMBRIDGE MUSIC HANDBOOKS

GENERAL EDITOR   Julian Rushton

Dowland: *Lachrimae* (1604)

Peter Holman

PUBLISHED BY THE PRESS SYNDICATE OF THE UNIVERSITY OF CAMBRIDGE
The Pitt Building, Trumpington Street, Cambridge, United Kingdom

CAMBRIDGE UNIVERSITY PRESS
The Edinburgh Building, Cambridge CB2 2RU, UK   http://www.cup.cam.ac.uk
40 West 20th Street, New York NY 10011-4211, USA   http://www.cup.org
10 Stamford Road, Oakleigh, Melbourne 3166, Australia

First published 1999

Printed in the United Kingdom at the University Press, Cambridge

Typeset in Ehrhardt MT 10½/13pt, in QuarkXPress™   [SE]

A catalogue record for this book is available from the British Library

Library of Congress cataloguing in publication data

Holman, Peter
Dowland, *Lachrimae* (1604) / Peter Holman.
p.   cm. – (Cambridge music handbooks)
Includes bibliographical references and index.
ISBN 0 521 58196 6 (hardback). – ISBN 0 521 58829 4 (paperback)
1. Dowland, John, 1563?–1626. *Lachrimae.* I. Title. II. Series.
ML410.D808H65   1999
784.18′82–dc21   98-54374   CIP   MN

ISBN 0 521 58196 6 hardback
ISBN 0 521 58829 4 paperback

In memory of
Robert Spencer
1932–1997

Contents

Contents

Note to the reader

Original written sources have been transcribed without changing spelling, capitalisation or punctuation, though I have not retained the contemporary distinctions between italic, black letter and roman type in printed documents, and I have modernised the interchangeable letters 'i' and 'j', 'u' and 'v'. Readers should be alert to the possibility that quotations taken from secondary sources might have been modernised more radically. All printed books were published in London unless otherwise stated. Pitches are indicated using the system in which the open strings of the viol family are D–G–c–e–a–d', G–c–f–a–d'–g' and d–g–c'–e'–a'–d''. Clefs are indicated using the system in which the treble, alto and bass clefs appear as g2, c3 and F4. I have modernised the English system of reckoning the year from Lady Day (25 March), and have used an asterisk to indicate those dates in documents that may have been reckoned using the 'New Style' or Gregorian calendar, instituted by Pope Gregory XIII in 1582 and rapidly adopted on the Continent. It was ten days ahead of the 'Old Style' or Julian calendar used at the time in England.

Abbreviations

(based on those used in *Grove 6*)

CCM	*John Dowland: Complete Consort Music*, ed. E. Hunt (London, 1985)
CLM	*The Collected Lute Music of John Dowland*, ed. D. Poulton and B. Lam (London, 3/1981)
CMM	Corpus mensurabilis musicae
DM	J. M. Ward, *A Dowland Miscellany*, *JLSA* 10 (1977)
Edwards	W. Edwards, introduction to the Boethius Press facsimile of *Lachrimae* (Leeds, 1974), reissued with additional material by S. McCoy and R. Spencer for the Severinus Press facsimile (Newbury, 1992)
EECM	Early English Church Music
EM	*Early Music*
Fiddlers	P. Holman, *Four and Twenty Fiddlers: The Violin at the English Court 1540–1690* (Oxford, 2/1995)
FoMRHIQ	*FoMRHI [Fellowship of Makers and Researchers of Historical Instruments] Quarterly*
Grove 6	*The New Grove Dictionary of Music and Musicians*, ed. S. Sadie, 20 vols. (London, 1980)
GSJ	*The Galpin Society Journal*
JAMIS	*Journal of the American Musical Instrument Society*
JAMS	*Journal of the American Musicological Society*
JD	D. Poulton, *John Dowland* (London, 2/1982)
JLSA	*Journal of the Lute Society of America*
LSJ	*The Lute Society Journal*
MB	Musica Britannica
MD	*Musica disciplina*
ML	*Music and Letters*
MQ	*The Musical Quarterly*

PRMA	*Proceedings of the Royal Musical Association*
RMARC	*Royal Musical Association Research Chronicle*

Library sigla

(following the RISM system as used in *Grove 6*)

Austria
A-Wn	Österreichische Nationalbibliothek, Musiksammlung

Germany
D-Kl	Kassel, Murhardsche Bibliothek der Stadt und Landesbibliothek
D-Mbs	Munich, Bayerische Staatsbibliothek

Great Britain
GB-Cfm	Cambridge, Fitzwilliam Museum
GB-Cu	Cambridge, University Library
GB-Ge	Glasgow, Euing Music Library
GB-Lam	London, Royal Academy of Music
GB-Lbl	London, British Library, Reference Division

United States of America
US-NH	New Haven, Yale University, School of Music Library
US-Ws	Washington, Folger Shakespeare Libraries

Preface

John Dowland used the Latin word 'Lachrimae' ('Tears') to mean three distinct but related things. First, it is the title of his famous pavan, best known as a solo lute piece but also surviving in many contemporary adaptations for other solo instruments or groups of instruments. Second, it is the title appended to Dowland's adaptation of the pavan as a song for two voices and lute, 'Flow my teares', published in *The Second Booke of Songs or Ayres* (1600). Third, the pavan, now entitled 'Lachrimae Antiquae', is the first item of the subject of this book, the collection Dowland published in London in the spring of 1604 as *Lachrimae, or Seaven Teares Figured in Seaven Passionate Pavans, with Divers other Pavans, Galiards, and Almands, Set Forth for the Lute, Viols, or Violons, in Five Parts*. In what follows I use 'Lachrimae' generally to mean the pavan in its various settings, 'Antiquae' specifically to mean its five-part setting as printed in the 1604 collection, and *Lachrimae* to mean the collection as a whole.

Lachrimae is a typeset folio volume in table layout, with the parts of each piece laid out around a single opening. It contains twenty-one pieces, ten pavans followed by nine galliards and two almands, each with staff-notation parts for five viols or violin-family instruments and a part in tablature for the lute. I list their titles as they appear in the body of the volume (there are some small differences in the way they are styled in the table of contents and between the parts), together with the abbreviations used in this book:

1 Lachrimae Antiquae	Antiquae
2 Lachrimae Antiquae Novae	Antiquae Novae
3 Lachrimae Gementes	Gementes
4 Lachrimae Tristes	Tristes

5	Lachrimae Coactae	Coactae
6	Lachrimae Amantis	Amantis
7	Lachrimae Verae	Verae
8	Semper Dowland semper Dolens	Dolens
9	Sir Henry Umptons Funerall	Unton
10	M. John Langtons Pavan	Langton
11	The King of Denmarks Galiard	Denmark
12	The Earle of Essex Galiard	Essex
13	Sir John Souch his Galiard	Souch
14	M. Henry Noel his Galiard	Noel
15	M. Giles Hobies his Galiard	Hoby
16	M. Nicholas Gryffith his Galiard	Gryffith
17	M. Thomas Collier his Galiard with 2 Trebles	Collier
18	Captaine Digorie Piper his Galiard	Piper
19	M. Buctons Galiard	Bucton
20	Mistresse Nichols Almand	Nichol
21	M. George Whitehead his Almand	Whitehead

There is still no satisfactory modern edition of *Lachrimae*. The first, edited by Peter Warlock for Oxford University Press (London, 1927), was, not surprisingly, intended for modern strings: it is laid out for the same combination as Schubert's C major String Quintet (two violins, viola and two cellos), the note-values of the pavans and galliards are halved, and it does not include the lute tablature. The edition by F. J. Giesbert, *Lachrimae oder sieben Tränen* (Kassel, 1954), includes the tablature but only consists of the seven 'Lachrimae' pavans. The most recent edition, by Edgar Hunt for Schott (London, 1985), includes *Lachrimae* in a supposedly *Complete Consort Music [CCM]* of Dowland, though it does not print the tablature, has no critical commentary, and is disturbingly inaccurate in places. There is an urgent need for a proper critical edition that includes the tablature, and takes account of variants between the six surviving copies of the publication and the various manuscript sources. In this book, bar numbers refer to the Hunt edition.

For those who can cope with the original notation and can manage to use the table layout, there are three facsimile editions. Boethius Press issued the copy in the Henry Watson Music Library, Manchester (Leeds, 1974), with an excellent brief survey by Warwick Edwards of the bibliographical and musical issues. Edwards's introduction was revised with additional material by Stewart McCoy and the late Robert Spencer for the publication by Severinus Press (Newbury, 1992) of the copy formerly in Robert Spencer's Library, now in the library of the Royal Academy of Music [Edwards]. Most recently, Performers' Facsimiles have reproduced the copy in the British Library (New York, 1998).

The reader wanting to study *Lachrimae* seriously will need to compare Dowland's consort settings with the various song and lute versions. The song books, *The First Booke* (1597), *The Second Booke* (1600), *The Third and Last Booke* (1603) and *A Pilgrimes Solace* (1612), as well as Robert Dowland's *A Musicall Banquet* (1610), were reprinted in facsimile by Scolar Press in the series *The English Lutesongs 1597–1632* (Menston, 1968–71). Versions for solo voice and lute were published by Edmund Fellowes in the series *The English School of Lutenist Song Writers* (1922–4), and were revised by Thurston Dart and David Scott between 1965 and 1969 in the series *The English Lute Songs*; *A Musicall Banquet* was edited complete for the first time by Peter Stroud for this series in 1968. The part-song versions were edited by Edmund Fellowes, Thurston Dart and Nigel Fortune as *Ayres for Four Voices*, MB 6 (1953; 2/1963; 3/1970). *The Collected Lute Music of John Dowland* was edited by Diana Poulton and Basil Lam (1974; 2/1978; 3/1981).

By and large, writers on Dowland (and Elizabethan music in general, for that matter) have been more concerned with biography and source studies than with writing about the music. This is true of Diana Poulton's pioneering *John Dowland* [*JD*] (London, 1972; 2/1982), though she offered some useful comments on the texts of the *Lachrimae* pieces and their relationship to other settings. John Ward's *A Dowland Miscellany* [*DM*], the complete *JLSA* 10 (1977), is largely a series of glosses on Poulton's book, and therefore shares her preoccupations.

For this reason, I have kept discussion of biographical and textual issues to a minimum, leaving as much space as possible for other things. Chapter 1 deals with *Lachrimae* as a document, investigating its publication history and the implications of its format, while Chapter 2 considers its instrumentation. Chapter 3 provides a context for understanding its place in the history of Renaissance dance music. Chapter 4 is concerned with the seven 'Lachrimae' pavans, and with the questions of meaning, musical context and intellectual background they pose. They are difficult questions, and scholars have mostly avoided trying to answer them, though I am most grateful to Dr Lionel Pike for letting me read the relevant portions of his unpublished book *Expression and the Evolution of Musical Language*, and to David Pinto for allowing me to refer to his article 'Dowland's Tears: Aspects of *Lachrimae*' prior to its publication in *The Lute*. Chapter 5 deals with the 'divers other Pavans, Galiards, and Almands', considering the significance of the dedications to Dowland's friends and patrons, and whether the collection as a whole has any coherence. Chapter 6 is a brief survey of Dowland's influence on succeeding generations, and the process of revival in modern times.

A book of this sort is inevitably heavily indebted to the work of others. My primary debt is to Robert Spencer. He put his unrivalled knowledge of Dowland at my disposal, and generously spent time and precious reserves of energy in the last months of his life reading successive drafts of the first two chapters and finding material for me in his magnificent library. I am grateful to Tim Carter, Tim Crawford, Ian Harwood, Lionel Pike, David Pinto, Rudolf Rasch, Richard Rastall, Julian Rushton, Matthew Spring and Peter Van Heyghen for reading drafts in whole or part, improving it greatly with their detailed criticism. Also, I must thank my daughter Sally for preparing the index, and Clifford Bartlett, Peter Berg, Alison Crum, Charles Foster, Robin Leaver, Paul O'Dette, Judy Tarling and Christopher R. Wilson for helping me in various ways.

1

The document

English music publishing

Music publishing came late to England.[1] While substantial trades developed in Venice, Paris, Nuremberg and Antwerp in the first half of the sixteenth century, virtually no music was published in London until the 1570s, apart from liturgical books with plainsong and collections of metrical psalms. It is not entirely clear why England lagged so far behind the Continent, though Queen Elizabeth tried to improve matters by granting two monopolies, one in 1559 to John Day for psalm books, and the other in 1575 for twenty-one years to Thomas Tallis and William Byrd for polyphonic music. The latter covered 'set songe or songes in partes, either in English, Latin, Frenche, Italian, or other tongues that may serve for musicke either in Church or chamber, or otherwise to be either plaid or soonge', as well as 'any paper to serve for printing or pricking any songe or songes' and 'any printed bokes or papers of any songe or songes, or any bookes or quieres of such ruled paper imprinted'.[2]

Tallis and Byrd used their monopoly to produce *Cantiones quae ab argumento sacrae vocantur* (1575), printed by Thomas Vautrollier, though it did not sell well and they appealed to Elizabeth in June 1577 for support, claiming they were out of pocket to the tune of at least 200 marks. Only two sets of part-books were issued before 1588, when Byrd, now sole holder, assigned it to the printer Thomas East. It was East who began the large-scale publication of polyphonic music, starting with *Musica transalpina* and Byrd's *Psalms, Sonets and Songs*. The Byrd–East monopoly expired in 1596, which provided openings for others. William Barley immediately produced *A New Book of Tabliture*, the first English printed collection of songs and solo music for lute, orpharion and bandora, while Peter Short started in 1597 with, among other things,

Thomas Morley's *Plaine and Easie Introduction to Practicall Musicke*, Anthony Holborne's *Cittharn Schoole*, Morley's *Canzonets or Little Short Aers to Five and Sixe Voices*, and Dowland's *First Booke of Songes or Ayres*.

The publication of Dowland's *First Booke* was a notable event. Short entered it in the Stationers' Register together with Morley's *Canzonets* on 31 October 1597, and the two collections share the distinction of being the first English prints of polyphonic vocal music with a tablature part.[3] *The First Booke* was highly successful: it was reprinted at least four times up to 1613, and its table layout (see below) was the model for all subsequent lute song collections.

With such a success on his hands, Peter Short must have been disappointed when, in the next year (1598), he was suddenly unable to print any more music. On 28 September Thomas Morley was granted a renewal of the music monopoly on similar terms as before, and for the same period, twenty-one years.[4] For some reason, Morley chose William Barley as his partner rather than East or Short, the two main London music printers. But on 29 May 1600 East was also authorised to print music for three years, and about the same time Short produced some volumes 'with the assent of Thomas Morley', including Robert Jones's *First Booke of Songes and Ayres* (1600), or at 'the assigne of Th. Morley', in the case of the 1600 reprint of Dowland's *First Booke*. But this sensible arrangement did not last long. Morley died in September or October 1602, and though his wife Susan inherited his estate she either died soon after or did not exercise her claim to the monopoly, and it effectively went into abeyance after East's three-year licence expired in May 1603. Moreover James I, the new king, created more uncertainty when, by a proclamation dated 7 May 1603, he suspended all monopolies pending an investigation of the subject.

Dowland's continental career

When *Lachrimae* appeared Dowland had been working abroad for a decade.[5] He had left England in 1594 after failing to obtain a vacant post as a court lutenist. After working briefly at Wolfenbüttel and Kassel, he left Germany for Italy to study with the Roman composer Luca Marenzio. According to a letter he wrote to Sir Robert Cecil from Nuremberg on 10 November 1595* (see Chapter 4), he got as far as Florence, where he was drawn into a group of English Catholics involved in plotting against Queen Elizabeth. He protested his innocence to Cecil, claiming that he quickly realised the seriousness of his position and returned to Germany, though the English authorities probably continued to regard him with suspicion. He certainly failed a second time to obtain an English court post during a visit in 1597, when he took the opportunity to publish *The First Booke*, and on 18 November 1598* he entered the service of Christian IV of Denmark.

Dowland was evidently highly valued by Christian IV. His salary of 500 Daler (more than £200 in contemporary English money) made him one of the highest paid court servants; his successor, Thomas Cutting, only received 300 Daler a year. He also received occasional gifts from the king, and was allowed extended periods of leave in England. The first visit occurred over the autumn, winter and spring of 1601–2, and was made to recruit musicians and purchase instruments. Dowland's second journey from Denmark to England occurred sometime between 15 July 1603*, when he received his salary up to 18 August*, and 10 July 1604*, when he was given arrears of pay up to 18 August* with the proviso that:

> it depends on His Royal Majesty's gracious pleasure whether His Majesty will be pleased to grant him the same salary, in view of the fact that he has travelled to England on his own business and remained there a long while, longer than His Royal Majesty had granted him leave of absence. And in case His Royal Majesty will not grant [part] of the same salary, he shall do future service therefore, or give satisfaction to His Royal Majesty therefore in other ways.

He must have still been in London on 9 May 1604, the day he wrote out a lute piece for a foreign visitor, Hans von Bodeck of Elbing (now Elblag in Poland).[6]

The publication of *Lachrimae*

It is often thought that Dowland made the 1603–4 journey to England specifically to publish *Lachrimae*, but his main motive seems to have been to lobby James I for the court post he had repeatedly failed to obtain from Queen Elizabeth. Indeed, he probably began to make preparations for the trip soon after the news of Elizabeth's death on 24 March 1603 reached Denmark. He clearly planned to approach James through the queen, Anne of Denmark, sister of his employer Christian IV, using *Lachrimae* to attract her attention. He dedicated it to Anne, and a close reading of the graceful dedication reveals a good deal about his plans and activities in the months before it was published:

> Since I had accesse to your Highnesse at Winchester (most gracious Queene) I have been twice under sayle for Denmarke, hastning my returne to my most royall King and Master, your deare and worthiest Brother; but by contrary windes and frost, I was forst backe againe, and of necessitie compeld to winter here in your most happie Kingdome. In which time I have endevoured by my poore labour and study to manifest my humblenesse and dutie to your highnesse, being my selfe one of your most affectionate Subjects, and also servant to your most Princely Brother, the onely Patron and Sun-shine of my else unhappie Fortunes. For which respects I have presumed to Dedicate this worke of Musicke to your sacred hands, that was begun where you were borne, and ended where you raigne. And though the title doth promise teares, unfit guests in these joyfull times, yet no doubt pleasant are the teares which Musicke weepes, neither are teares shed always in sorrowe, but sometime in joy and gladnesse. Vouchsafe then (worthy Goddesse) your Gracious protection to these showers of Harmonie, least if you frowne on them, they bee Metamorphosed into true teares.

We learn from this that Dowland was in England by the middle of September 1603: the queen arrived in Winchester on the 18th and stayed there until late October. The entertainment during her visit included a masque on 17 October – in which, perhaps, he played.[7] He wrote that he 'had accesse' to the queen at Winchester, which implies that he spoke to her in person, presumably requesting permission to dedicate *Lachrimae* to her and perhaps hinting that he was interested in a court post. His original plan was to return to Denmark before the winter, but he left it too late: he was 'twice under sayle' before 'contrary windes and frost' forced him to spend the winter in England. His statement that *Lachrimae* was 'begun where you were borne, and ended where you raigne' could mean that it was unfinished when he left Denmark, and needed 'labour and study' that winter in England to finish it, a point developed in Chapter 2.

If so, then Dowland could hardly have come to England in 1603 to see *Lachrimae* through the press. Had he returned to Denmark according to plan it is unlikely he would have had time to finish it before his departure, and he would have had to send the manuscript to London by post, as he had done with his two previous collections. The dedication of *The Second Booke of Songs or Ayres* to Lucy, Countess of Bedford is signed 'From Helsingnoure in Denmarke the first of June. 1600'*, and we know from a complicated series of lawsuits (discussed below) that the publisher purchased the collection from Dowland's wife in London. Also, Dowland remarked in the preface to his *Third and Last Booke of Songs or Aires* (1603) that it had been 'fetcht far from home, and brought even through the most perilous seas'; it was registered at Stationers' Hall on 21 February 1603, when he was certainly in Denmark.[8]

Lachrimae was entered by Thomas Adams in the Stationers' Register on 2 April 1604,[9] but there is no mention of him on the title-page: it was just 'Printed by John Windet, dwelling at the Signe of the Crosse Keyes at Powles Wharfe', and 'solde at the Authors house in Fetter-lane neare Fleet-streete'. Windet and Adams had both taken advantage of the hiatus in the music monopoly to become involved in publishing music. Windet had started printing psalm books in 1592 using John Day's old music type, which may have originated in Antwerp.[10] He began printing secular polyphonic music with *Lachrimae* and Thomas Greaves's *Songes of Sundrie Kindes* (both entered in the Stationers' Register on the same day) and continued with a number of part-book and table layout collections over the next three years, by Richard Alison, John Bartlet, John Coprario, Michael East, Thomas Ford, Tobias Hume and Robert Jones. Windet began to use a new fount when he turned to secular music. Like several others used at the time by London printers, it was modelled on the one Vautrollier seems to have obtained from Pierre Haultin in La Rochelle, though Windet mixed in pieces from the Day fount and, probably, other sources; the most obvious sign of this in *Lachrimae* is the apparently incongruous use of several types of sharps and flats on the same page.[11]

The tablature type used by Windet in *Lachrimae* and his other table layout books is essentially that used by William Barley in Alison's *Psalmes of David in Meter* (1599) and Morley's *First Booke of Ayres* (1600), and was apparently borrowed by Windet from Barley; Barley used it again in Thomas Robinson's *New Citharen Lessons* (1609).[12] *Lachrimae* differs from the other examples of the Barley–Windet tablature in its extensive use of beamed rhythm flags, which presumably reflects Dowland's own preference. They also appear in the autograph sections of the Dowland Lutebook in Washington and the Board Manuscript, though oddly not in any of his song books.[13] William Chappell claimed in 1844 that Edward Rimbault was 'in possession of a portion of the original manuscript', though it does not appear in the catalogue of Rimbault's library, sold in 1877, and does not seem to survive.[14]

Thomas Adams had been a bookseller and publisher at the White Lion in St Paul's Churchyard from 1591, but started publishing music in 1603 taking advantage of the hiatus in the music monopoly. He began with Dowland's *Third and Last Booke* and a reprint of *The First Booke*, and went on to issue Dowland's translation of *Andreas Ornithoparcus his Micrologus* (1609), and Robert Dowland's anthologies *Varietie of Lute-Lessons* (1610) and *A Musicall Banquet* (1610), as well as collections by John Danyel and Thomas Ravenscroft. It seems that Dowland had also planned to use Adams to publish *Lachrimae*, but changed his mind, perhaps because his enforced stay in England gave him the time to organise its sale himself, and he thought he could make more money that way.

Perhaps Dowland came to this conclusion by hearing about the complicated and protracted series of lawsuits relating to the publication of *The Second Booke* between the publisher George Eastland and Thomas East.[15] He would doubtless have been interested to learn that Eastland printed 1000 copies (the largest run allowed by the Stationers' Company) and planned to sell them at 4s 6d each. Thus Eastland stood to make as much as £225 against expenses he estimated at £100, but East described that sum as 'such apparent an untruth', and submitted a more detailed and convincing estimate of only £47 12s. It reveals that Dowland's wife received £20 'for the manuscript and half the dedication' – that is, half the reward that could be expected from the queen for the dedication. No wonder Dowland was tempted to publish *Lachrimae* himself.

Lachrimae was published without a date, though the copies in Manchester Public Library and the British Library have the dates 1605 and 1605 or possibly 1606 added by hand to the title-page.[16] 1605 was accepted by earlier scholars, but both dates were apparently added relatively recently and have no authority; the entry in the Stationers' Register makes it clear it appeared in the spring of 1604. But scholars do not seem to have asked themselves why *Lachrimae* is one of the very few undated typeset music prints from Elizabethan and Jacobean England. To answer the question we must return to the tangled and uncertain situation in the music publishing trade.

With the litigation surrounding *The Second Booke* fresh in his mind, it is easy to see why Dowland might have chosen to disguise the fact that it had appeared without the authorisation of the holder of the monopoly or an assignee at a period when the ownership of the monopoly was in question. He was perhaps wise to be cautious, for in May 1606 and October 1609 William Barley won court cases against East and Adams, claiming an interest in the monopoly as Morley's former partner.[17] Dowland might also have decided to leave the date off the title-page of *Lachrimae* because he was not sure how long he would be in England, when he would return, or how well the collection would sell in his absence. It would have been easier to dispose of the stock over a period if it was not obvious on the title-page that it was no longer a novelty. For a similar reason, most engraved editions issued by eighteenth-century English music publishers are undated: it allowed them to run off more copies as and when demand arose without revealing the age of the publication, and without having to change the title-page.

The table layout

The normal way of publishing polyphonic vocal or instrumental music was in sets of quarto part-books, with each book containing all the parts in the collection for a particular instrument or voice range. But *The First Booke* is a folio intended to be placed flat on a small table, to be read by the performers grouped around it. Each piece is laid out on a single opening, with the Cantus and the lute tablature underlaid on the left-hand page, and the other three vocal parts grouped around the three sides of the right-hand page.

One of the attractions of the table layout was its flexibility. Since each opening could be laid out differently, it was easy to include a wide variety of music, including solo songs, part-songs, madrigals, masque music and even anthems and motets, while Dowland developed a type of part-song for the format that could be used in many different ways. All the songs in

The First Booke can be performed by a single person singing the tune and playing the underlaid tablature on the left-hand page. Alternatively, they can be sung as part-songs with or without the lute, using some or all of the lower parts on the right-hand page, or with viols replacing or doubling some or all of the voices. It was an elegant solution to the problem of printing music with a tablature part as well as staff notation. Morley's *Canzonets*, its competitor, inspired no imitations, probably partly because it was a set of part-books with the tablature printed inconveniently on separate pages of the Cantus – requiring two copies for performance.[18]

The table layout was not entirely Dowland's invention. GB-Lbl, Add. MS 31390, a large manuscript dated 1578 of 'In Nomines & other solfainge Songes' for 'voyces or Instrumentes', has the parts of each piece spread around the four sides of each opening.[19] Similar formats had already been used in continental publications. Jacques Moderne printed four-part pieces in *Le parangnon des chansons* (Lyons, 1538–43) on a single opening, with two of the parts upside-down at the top of the page, while the lute duets in Pierre Phalèse's *Hortus musarum* and *Luculentum theatrum musicum* (Louvain, 1552, 1568) are arranged so that the players sit facing each other; in *Florilegium* by Adrian Denss (Cologne, 1594), the lutenist sits opposite the singers.[20] Similarly, in an Elizabethan lute song manuscript, GB-Lbl, Add. MS 4900, the performers sit facing one another or at right angles.

Of course, the table layout is related to the choirbook format, in which all the parts of a polyphonic vocal piece are spread around a single opening but face the same direction; the book is placed on a lectern or music desk rather than flat on a table. It was used in some continental vocal collections with tablature parts, such as Emanuel Adriaenssen's *Pratum musicum* and *Novum pratum musicum* (Antwerp, 1584, 1592), and the *Canzonette a tre voci* (Venice, 1596) by Alessandro Orologio, the Prague-based wind player Dowland met at Kassel in 1594.[21] A similar format is used for the two fantasias for cittern and/or three single-line instruments in Holborne's *Cittharn Schoole*.[22] Dowland's innovation was to apply the full table layout of Add. MS 31390, with parts laid around all four sides of the book, to a printed collection and to flexible combinations of voices and lute.

Lachrimae is modelled on *The First Booke* and other lute-song collections in table layout. It is also a folio book, with the parts for each piece distributed around the sides of a single opening in the following order: Cantus (left bottom), Bassus (left middle, facing outwards), Quintus (left top, upside down), Tenor (right top, upside down), the lute tablature (right middle, opposite the Bassus), and Altus (right bottom) (see Fig. 1.1). Dowland presumably chose the table layout for *Lachrimae* because it had been so successful in *The First Booke*. But he may also have been trying to avoid an obvious problem with conventional part-books: the tablature takes up more space than the other parts. The problem was avoided in Morley's *First Booke of Consort Lessons* (1599; 2/1611) and Philip Rosseter's *Lessons for Consort* (1609) by printing the lute part in folio and the others in quarto.[23] But this created another problem: the sets did not have a consistent format, and so there was a danger that the lute part would get separated from the others, or would have to be folded across the middle to fit on a shelf with them, risking damage. This is perhaps why we have no example of the two editions of Morley's lute part and only a few fragments of a single copy of Rosseter's; significantly, they show signs of having been folded.[24]

But publishing consort music in table layout created its own problems. Dowland was aware that space round the table would be limited, for he placed the parts for the bass and lute, the largest instruments, on the sides of the opening facing in, so that they had the most room. But even so, experiment shows that it is difficult to get five viol players and a lutenist seated around a single table and a single copy of the collection: if they get close enough to read the music comfortably there is no room for bowing; if they withdraw to a comfortable distance the music is too small to read.[25] Of course, the same arguments apply to Add. MS 31390, but Warwick Edwards has argued, using the phrase 'solfainge Songes' in its title as evidence, that the Elizabethan instrumental ensemble repertory was used for singing as much as playing, particularly for didactic purposes in choir schools.[26] It is also possible that some of its pieces were intended for wind players, who, like singers, would have had less trouble than string players gathering around a single book. Another option for performers of *Lachrimae*, of course, was to buy more than one copy, and this is perhaps why two were included in the collection of English music prints purchased by a German nobleman in London in 1630, until recently in the library of Schlobitten Castle.[27]

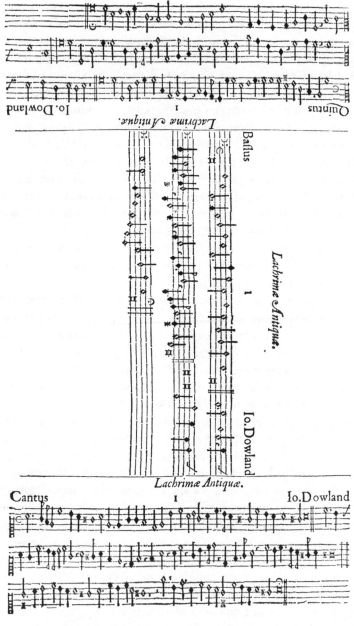

Fig. 1.1 The table layout: *Lachrimae*, sig. B1, B2

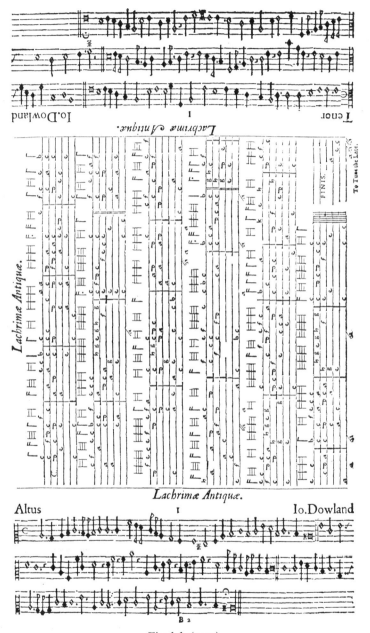

Fig. 1.1 *(cont.)*

11

All in all, *Lachrimae* does not seem to have been very successful. We do not know how well it sold, or how much money Dowland made out of it, but he never acted as his own publisher again, and it was never reprinted, despite his fame and the rarity of English publications of consort music; *Lachrimae* was only the third, after Morley's *Consort Lessons* and Anthony Holborne's *Pavans, Galliards, Almains* (1599).[28] The Prussian nobleman's purchase shows that there was still unsold stock in 1630, though this may tell us more about the embryonic nature of the English music trade than about how the collection was perceived by Dowland's contemporaries.[29] But no one repeated the experiment of printing consort music in table layout, and its music had little influence on English composers, who had begun to move on to other things by 1604. Doubtless Dowland was disappointed by the failure of *Lachrimae* to obtain him that coveted court post, though a sensible person would have realised that he was putting Queen Anne into an impossible position: she could hardly be seen to be poaching a servant of her brother. It was also perhaps unwise to have added the motto 'Aut Furit, aut Lachrimat, quem non Fortuna beavit' ('whom Fortune has not blessed, he either rages or weeps') on the title-page, for it might have been construed as a criticism of his employer. But common sense was not Dowland's strong point: as his friend Henry Peacham put it in *The Compleat Gentleman* (1622), he 'slipt many opportunities in advancing his fortunes'.[30]

2

The instruments

When John Dowland published *Lachrimae* he was contributing to a genre that was about a century old. The idea of developing instruments in several sizes to play polyphonic music, mimicking the ranges of the various voices of a vocal ensemble, seems to go back to the late fourteenth century, when a tenor-range bombard was developed from the soprano-range shawm. The flute, the recorder and the *douçaine* (probably a soft type of shawm) were developed in sets or consorts during the fifteenth century. But it was not until the 1490s that the idea was applied to bowed instruments.[1]

The viol consort was apparently developed in Brescia around 1495 on the orders of Isabella d'Este, the wife of Francesco Gonzaga, Duke of Mantua. The model was an existing tenor-sized bowed instrument recently imported into Italy from the Valencian area of Spain. The Valencian viol, like other mediaeval bowed instruments, only existed in a single size and had been used to play monophonic music using drone techniques with a flat bridge or no bridge at all. So to make it suitable for polyphonic music it had to be fitted with an arched bridge, and two other sizes were developed, making a consort of three. The violin consort was apparently developed in a similar fashion about a decade later at the neighbouring Este court in Ferrara by deriving a bass and a soprano from the alto-range vielle. The viol and the violin retained many of the characteristics of the parent instruments: the Valencian viol was a fairly large instrument held upright on the lap (*da gamba*), with a flat back and frets, while the vielle was a smaller instrument played on the shoulder (*da braccio*), with an arched back and no frets.

Thus, the viol was not the ancestor of the violin, as is often thought. The two families were invented at about the same time, for similar reasons but for different purposes. They provided the advanced humanist circle of the Estes and Gonzagas with an alternative to consorts of wind instruments. Following classical authors such as Plato and Aristotle, humanist thought regarded winds as less noble than strings, and the phallic associations of wind instruments also made them unsuitable for the patronage of female aristocrats such as Isabella d'Este and Lucrezia Borgia, Alfonso d'Este's wife. But they were used in different ways. Viols, soft, sonorous but rather lacking in attack, were suitable for serious contrapuntal music, while violins, louder, higher-pitched and more sprightly, were ideal for the new repertory of composed four-, five- and six-part dance music.

The viol and the violin spread with remarkable rapidity all over Europe in the first half of the sixteenth century. This was partly because they were perceived to be the best vehicles for the new repertories of polyphonic instrumental music, but it was also because they were typically played by self-sufficient and mobile groups of professional musicians based on one or two families, who recruited their own personnel, composed or arranged their own repertory, and often made their own instruments. The viol was probably brought to the English court around 1515 by members of the van Wilder family from The Netherlands, and their consort was superseded there in 1540 by a six-man group made up of three families of Sephardic Jews from Venice, Milan and Brescia who played violins as well as viols.[2] The ensemble they founded served successive English monarchs from Henry VIII to Charles I, and formed the nucleus of the Twenty-four Violins in Charles II's reign.

The viol and the violin apparently began to appear in English aristocratic households in the 1530s and the 1560s respectively, and were taken up by waits (town musicians) and humbler professionals several decades later.[3] There were sufficient instrumentalists at court to allow a group to specialise in stringed instruments, but musicians elsewhere had to be more versatile. 'R. B.', the author of the treatise 'Some Rules and Orders for the Government of an Earle' (*c.* 1605), thought that an earl should employ five musicians for the following duties:

> At greate feastes when the Earles service is going to the table they are to play upon Shagbutts, Cornetts, Shalmes, and such other instruments going with winde. In meale times to play upon vialls, violens or other[wise] broken musicke. They are to teach the Earles children to singe and play upon the base violl the virginalls, Lute, Bandora, or Citerne.[4]

R. B. assumed that professionals would play the main sets of ensemble instruments but would teach the children of the house solo instruments. In Mantua and Ferrara aristocrats had played in the earliest viol consorts, but in England the more advanced skills required for playing in ensembles were not generally cultivated by amateurs until the reign of James I. In Elizabethan England the viol was almost as closely associated with professionals as the violin.

For this reason, only a few publications of consort music appeared in England during Dowland's lifetime, and we should not assume that they were aimed exclusively at the amateur market. Anthony Holborne advertised *Pavans, Galliards, Almains* (1599) as suitable 'for Viols, Violins, or Other[wise] Musicall Winde Instruments', which recalls the list of instruments R. B. recommended for household musicians. Dedicating the collection to Sir Richard Champernowne of Modbury in south Devon, Holborne wrote that it contained 'a more liberall and enlarged choice then hath at any time as yet come to your refined eares'. Thus it seems that the collection was partly written for Champernowne's household musicians, and that his role was as a listener rather than participant.[5] Obvious purchasers would have been those professional groups that did not have a skilled composer or arranger at their disposal.

Nor should we assume that Holborne intended the instruments he lists to be mixed together. The normal practice of professional groups was to use them as alternatives in a musical menu rather than as ingredients in a single dish. They would have used wind instruments outdoors and (as R. B. suggests) in processions, viols for *Tafelmusik*, and violins for the dancing that regularly followed Elizabethan meals. Loud wind bands often mixed shawms, sackbuts and curtals, but the only established mixed ensemble of soft instruments in Elizabethan England was the six-man group of treble viol or violin, tenor flute or recorder, bass viol, lute, cittern and bandora, used in Morley's *Consort Lessons*, Rosseter's *Lessons for Consort*, and several manuscript sources.[6] But this genre, with three parts in tablature and only three in staff notation, was quite distinct from the main repertory of five- and six-part staff-notation music, and was regarded as something of an exotic musical luxury. Charles Butler wrote as late as 1636 that 'The several kinds of Instruments ar commonly used severally by them selves: as a Set of Viols, a Set of Waits [shawms], or the like', but added: 'sometimes, upon some special occasion, many of both Sorts ar moste sweetely joined in Consort'.[7] Thus we should think twice about playing five-part dance music of the sort published by Holborne with mixed ensembles. Everything we know about sixteenth-century instrumentation suggests that it was intended for five instruments of the same family.

Lachrimae and the Anglo-German repertory

The same arguments apply to *Lachrimae*. It is a collection of five-part dance music, and it has a similar formula on the title-page: 'set forth for the Lute, Viols, or Violons, in five parts'. But Dowland did not include 'Musicall Winde Instruments', and it is worth considering why. It was presumably partly because he was aware of the potential problems of combining wind instruments with a lute (a point to which we will return), but it was also because *Lachrimae* is to some extent more typical of consort music written by English musicians on the Continent than of English consort music: Dowland's phrase in the dedication that *Lachrimae* 'was begun where you were borne, and ended where you raigne' seems to mean that some of the pieces were written for court musicians in Denmark.

Dowland was not the only English musician to work at the Danish court. Several groups had been there in the 1580s, and those who were there with him include William Brade (1594–6, 1599–1606), John Meinert or Myners (1599–1601), Daniel Norcombe (1599–1601), the dancing master Henry Sandam (1601–2), and Bendix or Benedictus Greebe or Grep (1595–1619), who was perhaps an Englishman, Benedict Greeve or Greaves, and the harpist 'Carolus Oralii' (1601–2), perhaps an Irishman, Charles O'Reilly. Dowland may have been recommended to Christian IV by one of them, or alternatively by his friend Alessandro Orologio, who had connections with the Danish court.

Christian IV was not alone in employing Englishmen. Between about 1580 and 1620 many musicians left England to work on the Continent. Some, like Peter Philips, Richard Deering, Daniel Norcombe and John Bull, were Catholic refugees from persecution. Others were members of theatre companies forced to tour abroad by the statute of 1572 that restricted the activities of 'Comon Players in Enterludes & Minstrels'.[8] Some, like the influential composers William Brade and Thomas

Simpson, were apparently just attracted by the possibility of lucrative employment in the prosperous cities and small courts of Germany and Scandinavia. Many were string players. The five Englishmen who came from Copenhagen in 1586 to work in Dresden were *Geiger* (fiddlers), and were partly hired to 'entertain and play music on their *Geygen* and instruments of such like' during meals, while an account of a theatre group that arrived in Kassel in 1601 refers to their *Saitenspiel* (string playing).[9] Brade called himself 'Violist und Musicus' and 'Fiolist und Musicum' on the title-pages of his 1609 and 1614 collections, while Simpson described himself as 'Violisten und Musicum' on the title-pages of his three collections.[10]

These *émigrés* developed an Anglo-German repertory that was founded on English consort music, but differed from it in several respects. Since most of it was the work of string players rather than organists or choir masters, it consisted of dance music rather than fantasias, and was focused particularly on sets of violins or viols. Some collections, such those published by Zacharius Füllsack and Christian Hildebrand in 1607 and 1609, by Simpson in 1610, and by Brade in 1614 and 1617, use variants of the phrase 'auff allerley Instrumenten und insonderheit auff Fiolen zu gebrauchen' ('for various instruments, and particularly suitable for strings'), though they were rarely as specific as Bartolomeus Praetorius, with the formula 'auf der Figoli Gamba und Figoli di Braccia artlich zu gebrauchen' in his *Newe liebliche Paduanen und Galliarden* (Berlin, 1616).[11] Michael Praetorius wrote in 1618–19 that town musicians call viols *Violen* and violins *Geigen* or *Polnische Geigen*, though there is evidence that, in the Anglo-German repertory at least, *Violen* (or *Fiolen*) was used like the parent Italian word *viole* to mean violins as well as viols.[12]

Instrumentation

Nearly all treatises of the time give three tunings for the viol and violin families, not four.[13] For example, Giovanni Maria Lanfranco wrote in his *Scintille di musica* (Brescia, 1533) that when a *contralto* was used in the violin consort each string was 'made to resonate in unison with the Tenor', and that a *contralto* viol was tuned 'string by string in unison with the Tenor'.[14] Thus, four-part music laid out in the standard way with a single soprano, two inner parts and bass was played with a single violin, two violas, and a bass violin, or a treble viol, two tenor viols and a bass viol. The modern notion of a fourth size of violin, the so-called 'tenor violin', seems to derive from an implausible statement in Lodovico Zacconi's *Prattica di musica* (Venice, 1592), copied by Daniel Hitzler in *Extract aus der neuen Musica oder Singkunst* (Nuremberg, 1623), which allocates the tuning F–c–g–d' to the viola.[15] Praetorius gave it as a bass tuning, and it was probably used on small bass violins made to be played standing or walking along, slung across the chest and supported by a strap.[16] When a third inner part was added to the texture, as it generally was towards the end of the sixteenth century, then the extra part (or Quintus) was played on a third alto or tenor, not a second soprano or bass. Thus Mersenne wrote that the French court violin band, the *Vingt-quatre violons*, played in five parts with 'six trebles, six basses, four contratenors, four altos, and four of a fifth part'; the three inner parts were played by violas 'of different sizes, even though they are [tuned] in unison'.[17]

This exemplifies a basic principle of sixteenth-century instrumentation that is often ignored today: instruments are allocated according to function, so soprano instruments, such as the treble viol and the violin, only play soprano parts, bass instruments only play bass parts, and alto or tenor instruments only play inner parts – which is why the inner parts of *Lachrimae* and virtually all other consort music of the time never go below c, the lowest note of the viola and many tenor wind instruments. Thus Peter Warlock was wide of the mark when he scored his edition of *Lachrimae* for two violins, viola and two cellos. It should have been violin, three violas and bass violin – or on viols, treble, three tenors and bass.

Towards the end of the sixteenth century a new scoring developed in consort music, exemplified in *Lachrimae* by 'M. Thomas Collier his Galiard with 2 Trebles'. The Quintus was raised an octave from its normal tenor range, turning it into a Cantus Secundus that continually crosses and exchanges material with the Cantus. According to the principle of allocating instruments just explained, pieces using this scoring require two violins, two violas and bass violin, or two treble viols, two tenors and bass. When Dowland used the two-soprano scoring in 'Collier' he was conforming to German or Anglo-German, rather than English, practice. The two-soprano scoring seems to have come into German dance music from Italian madrigals and *balletti*, as well as from

Italianate vocal music by German composers. In Hans Leo Hassler's *Lustgarten neuer teutscher Gesäng* (Nuremberg, 1601), for instance, six-part intradas appear side-by-side with five-part German songs in a dance-like idiom derived from Gastoldi; both use the two-soprano scoring.[18]

More relevant to Dowland, Alessandro Orologio used the two-soprano scoring throughout his five- and six-part *Intradae*, a collection dedicated to Christian IV.[19] The scoring is also found in many Anglo-German sources, starting with D-Kl, 4° MS mus. 125, 1–5, a manuscript containing fifty-three five-part pavans apparently copied by an Englishman in Kassel around 1600, and the slightly later 4° MS mus. 72, 1–5, containing a number of pavans by the Landgrave of Hesse.[20] Later examples include pieces in the 1607 and 1609 Füllsack and Hildebrand anthologies, the 1610 and 1617 prints by Simpson, and the 1609, 1614, 1617 and 1621 prints by Brade. The two-soprano scoring does not seem to have been used in English five-part dance music until the second decade of the seventeenth century; the first examples are probably in GB-Lbl, Add. MSS 17786–91, apparently copied in Oxford by William Wigthorpe around 1615.[21]

I drew attention earlier to the phrase in the *Lachrimae* dedication that suggests the collection was partly written in Denmark and partly in England. I believe this explains an odd feature of the writing: the pieces can be divided by the range of their parts into two groups. The first, consisting of the seven 'Lachrimae' pavans, 'Dolens', 'Unton' and 'Souch', are generally low pitched and use the soprano (c1) clef for the Cantus part, which in several cases goes down to b or c'. The others lie rather higher, particularly in the upper parts, while the Cantus is in the treble (g2) clef, and never goes below d', with some pieces only going down to g'.

Why is this so? An obvious possibility is that one group was written in Denmark for performers at Christian IV's court, while the other was completed in England specifically for the publication. Dowland implies as much by describing *Lachrimae* in the preface as 'a long and troublesome worke, wherein I have mixed new songs with olde, grave with light'. If so, then the high-pitched pieces are likely to be the ones written in Denmark, for several reasons. They include most of the pieces known to have been written earlier as songs or lute solos, such as 'Essex', 'Noel' and 'Piper'. Among them is 'Collier', with its Anglo-German two-soprano scoring, as well as 'Denmark', dedicated to his employer Christian IV. Furthermore, the low-pitched group includes the seven 'Lachrimae' pavans, none of which exists in earlier versions – apart, of course, from 'Antiquae'. It is possible, even likely, that they were written at a late stage specifically for the publication, in England rather than Denmark. It raises the remarkable possibility that Dowland wrote his most sublime and complex works in relative haste during the winter of 1604–5.

Chiavette and transposition

Another possibility is that, in the form that they appear in *Lachrimae*, the two groups are intended for different instruments. Violins are smaller, livelier instruments than the equivalent sizes of viols, and work better playing higher-pitched music. In particular, the violin and the viola have smaller bodies and shorter string lengths, with bottom strings a fourth higher than their equivalents, the treble viol and the tenor viol. For this reason, in Italy violins were classed with cornetts as *stromenti acuti* that either transposed up low-tessitura music in low clefs or *chiavi naturali* (typically c1–c3–c4–F4), or played high-tessitura music in high clefs or *chiavette* (typically g2–c2–c3–c4 or F3) *come stà* – at pitch.[22] By contrast, the *stromenti coristi*, principally viols and recorders, used clef combinations in the same way as vocal ensembles: they played low clefs *come stà* but transposed *chiavette* pieces down; the interval traversed varied between a second and a fifth, but normally seems to have been a fourth.

In this way, it was possible to avoid the thin and unlovely upper register of the treble viol as well as the unsatisfactory bottom strings of the violin and the viola. Before metal wound strings were developed in the 1650s thick and unwieldy plain gut had to be used for their bottom strings, which were therefore avoided as much as possible in favour of their middle and upper registers. It is possible that other methods of increasing the density of strings without increasing their thickness, such as 'loading' them in copper solution or roping together several strands of gut, had been developed earlier, but we do not know whether they were used by musicians associated with Dowland, and the whole subject is controversial at present.[23]

It was also possible to increase the sonority of a viol consort by using a consort pitched a fourth or fifth lower than the standard one, using a tenor, two or three basses, and a great bass. Praetorius associated this device with the English, when they are 'playing viols on their own', and thought it sounded 'much more rich and majestic' than a consort 'tuned to the usual pitches'.[24] It is important, of course, not to confuse these transposing devices with the variations in pitch standard that existed at the time between different places, and between different types of ensemble. At present, it is not possible to draw any firm conclusions about the pitch standards used by Danish or English string consorts in the early seventeenth century, though they are likely to have been substantially lower than modern pitch or the various church and organ pitches of the time.[25] Wind instruments were usually made to play at high pitch, which may be one reason why Dowland did not specify them on the title-page of *Lachrimae*.

The musicians who developed the Anglo-German repertory evidently knew the *chiavette* system. The 1607 and 1609 Füllsack and Hildebrand anthologies, for instance, have five-part pieces in g2–g2–c2–c3–F3 as well as c1–c1–c3–c4–F4 clefs, as does Simpson's 1610 collection, while Simpson's violinistic 1617 collection is entirely in *chiavette*. But the repertory also includes many examples of mixed clefs, including the ones used in *Lachrimae*, c1 or g2–c2–c3–c4–F4, and, significantly, they are often applied to English pieces. Furthermore, g2–c2–c3–c4–F4 is used for most of Holborne's *Pavans, Galliards, Almains*, though some of the more sombre pavans, like Dowland's seven 'Lachrimae' pavans, have low-lying Cantus parts in c1. Ian Harwood has drawn attention to evidence of two pitch standards a fourth apart in English mixed consort music and related repertories, though there is little or no evidence of *chiavette* in the mainstream repertory of single-line consort music.[26] The contents of the two *Elizabethan Consort Music* volumes in Musica Britannica, for instance, are almost entirely in *chiavi naturali* or in mixed clefs; significantly, the main exceptions are three In Nomines by the Italian Alfonso Ferrabosco I, in g2–c1–c2–c3–F3 clefs.[27]

What does all this mean for *Lachrimae*? Though it does not divide into *chiavette* and *chiavi naturali* as clearly as some other Anglo-German collections, it could be that Dowland wrote the high-pitched group for a violin consort at the Danish court, and the low-pitched pieces with viols mainly in mind, specially for the publication. In practice, the low-pitched pieces gain from being transposed up a fourth when performed by a violin consort using plain gut strings, and there is some evidence that this was done at the time. 'Antiquae' is in A minor, as is 'Flow my teares', while most lute settings are in G minor. But a surprising number of settings in other media are in D minor, including those for keyboard by Byrd and Sweelinck, a five-part arrangement by William Wigthorpe, an incomplete Scottish one in Thomas Wode's part-books, and Morley's mixed consort arrangement.[28] The last three are probably examples of upward transposition in action, made to bring the soprano part into a good range for the violin.

The lute part

Lachrimae was the first collection of string consort music with a tablature part, though parts with a similar function were printed in some sixteenth-century collections of music for voices and lutes, while Orazio Vecchi's *Selva di varia ricreatione* (Venice, 1590) includes a 'Saltarello detto Trivella' for five-part 'Stromenti da corde' and lute in a collection of largely vocal music.[29] Furthermore, several pictures show lutes playing with violin consorts. Obvious examples are the illustration of a wedding banquet in Düsseldorf on 16 June 1585* with what seems to be a four-part violin consort, a virginal and a lute, and the painting *Courtiers of Queen Elizabeth* of about 1600 attributed to Marcus Gheeraerts the Elder, which seems to show a four-part violin consort and lute.[30] So the practice of accompanying string consorts with plucked instruments was not new in 1604.

The *Lachrimae* tablature part requires an ordinary tenor lute using the standard English tuning, G–c–f–a–d'–g', for the stopped courses. In solo music the tuning could be relative rather than absolute, founded on *Gamut* (treatises merely advise the player to tune the top string 'so high as you dare venture for breaking'), but in *Lachrimae* and other consort music it had to conform to the pitch of the rest of the ensemble.[31] Thus the *Lachrimae* tablature part confirms an absolute G tuning, assuming, of course, that the other instruments are not transposing from their written pitches. *Lachrimae* is the first English collection to require a nine-course lute with three diapasons tuned to various combinations of F, E, D and

C, though Antoine Francisque had already used a similar arrangement in *Le Trésor d'Orphée* (Paris, 1600; repr. 1973). Dowland probably started playing on a six-course lute with the three lowest courses strung in octaves, as recommended in Adrian Le Roy's *A Briefe and easye instru[c]tion to learne the tableture to conduct and dispose thy hande unto the Lute* (1568) (repeated as late as 1596 in Barley's *Newe Booke of Tabliture*), and wrote for a seven-course lute in his first three song books. He evidently favoured unison basses in later life, for he wrote of octave stringing in the *Varietie of Lute-Lessons* that 'amongst learned Musitions that custome is left, as irregular to the rules of Musicke'.

There has been controversy in modern times over the nature and the function of the *Lachrimae* lute part. The phrase 'set forth for the Lute, Viols, or Violons' on the title-page has sometimes been thought of as a list of alternatives, implying that the lute part could be played by itself or could be omitted in performances with viols or violins. Dowland referred to *Lachrimae* as 'my Lute-lessons' in the preface, and some of the tablature parts circulated as solos in manuscript; seven were even printed as such in Joachim van den Hove's *Delitae musicae* (Utrecht, 1612). A few of them, such as 'Dolens' and 'Unton', work well as solos, but this cannot have been Dowland's intention throughout, since the Cantus – the tune – is partly or entirely missing from the lute part of the high-pitched pieces.

However, a simple way of getting round that problem would be to add the Cantus and Bassus parts to the lute, making a trio texture similar to the five galliards for soprano and bass instruments with lute in Emanuel Adriaenssen's *Novum pratum musicum* (Antwerp, 1592; repr. 1977), or some of the dances in Fabritio Caroso's dance treatise *Nobiltà di dame* (Venice, 1600; repr. 1970).[32] More relevant to Dowland is van den Hove's *Praeludia testudinis, ad symphoniam duarum vocum duarumve violarum accomodata* (Leiden, 1616; repr. 1982),[33] and the sequence of eleven pavans for violin, bass violin and lute in *Le petit boucquet de frise orientale* ([?Emden], 1631; repr. 1987) by the Frisian lutenist Louis de Moy. De Moy's pavans partly belong to the Anglo-German tradition, and one of them alludes to 'Lachrimae'. Of course, Dowland himself published three songs in *A Pilgrimes Solace*, 'Goe nightly cares', 'From silent night' and 'Lasso vita mia', with accompaniments for lute and untexted Cantus and Bassus parts.

What, then, of the other possibility: that the lute could be omitted in consort performances? It is true that the tablature is largely confined to doubling the strings, except for the rhythmic patterns and ornamental flourishes that fill in the final bars of sections. But that is to be expected. The written-out lute parts in ensemble music of all types in the sixteenth and early seventeenth centuries normally double the parts they accompany. If they do not always double the top parts, as in the part-song versions of Dowland's lute songs or the high-pitched pieces in *Lachrimae*, then that may simply be because composers were unwilling to take the lute too high rather than because they were unwilling to double the tune. Everything we know about keyboard accompaniment at the time suggests that organists normally doubled all the parts of polyphonic vocal music or instrumental ensemble music, even in solo sonatas and trio sonatas.[34] The notion that continuo players should avoid the melodic lines they accompany seems to have developed at a much later period.

Nevertheless, there is nothing particularly sacrosanct about the lute parts in *Lachrimae*. It is easy to imagine that Dowland and other professional lutenists at the time would have embellished them on the repeats of the strains, producing something not unlike the lute parts of mixed consorts, with their written-out divisions. Indeed, a manuscript mixed consort lute part for 'Essex' can be used more or less as it stands with the *Lachrimae* setting.[35] Furthermore, a lutenist playing a normal 'mean' lute in G with a violin consort transposing the low-pitched pieces up a fourth would have had to devise his own lute part, though the tablature could have been played as it stood on a small 'treble' lute a fourth higher – the sort of instrument Ian Harwood has argued was used in the mixed consort repertory.[36] Similarly, a bass lute in D could theoretically have been used in performances with a low-pitched viol consort a fourth lower, though the large size of the instrument would have made the stretches difficult.

The instrumentation of *Lachrimae* is best understood as a small but significant step in the sequence of changes that was to transform the Anglo-German repertory in little more than a decade from what we think of as a late Renaissance idiom to an early Baroque one. Dowland took the first three steps by restricting the choice of instrument to strings, by adding an accompaniment to the full-voiced five-part texture, and by introducing an element of dialogue in one piece by turning the

Quintus into a second soprano. It was left to others such as Thomas Simpson and Samuel Scheidt to replace the lute tablature with a single-line continuo part, to increase the polarisation of the texture by reducing the number of inner parts, and to begin to write specifically and idiomatically for violins.

3

The dance types

The main courtly dances of the fifteenth century, collectively called *basse danse* or *bassadanza*, were typically accompanied by the *alta capella*, a loud wind ensemble in which stereotyped counterpoint was improvised around a slow-moving cantus firmus played by the tenor shawm or bombard. Since the length of each cantus firmus varied, each *basse danse* had its own choreography. The new dances that replaced it shortly after 1500 were much simpler. They had standard choreographies matched by simple tunes made up of short repeated sections in patterns such as AABB or AABBCC. The music, now increasingly intended for the new string consorts rather than the old loud wind ensembles, was usually in four, five or six parts using simple block chords, and had to be set down on paper, for the inner parts no longer had readily defined or discrete functions, and could not easily have been improvised without creating glaring consecutives. But dance music continued to be played from memory: pictures show groups performing without music for at least another century.

The pavan

The most important dances in the new repertory were those that make up most of *Lachrimae*, the pavan and the galliard. The *pavana* or *padoana* (the name suggests a connection with Padua or an allusion to the dignified display of the peacock by way of the Spanish *pavón*) is first found in Italian musical sources in the first decade of the sixteenth century, and spread rapidly to northern Europe. It seems to have arrived in England in the 1520s, for when the emperor Charles V danced 'la pabana' with some of his courtiers at Windsor on 15 June 1522 during his second visit to England, Henry VIII sat it out because, John Ward has suggested, he was unfamiliar with it. Yet it had joined the list of current dances by the time Sir Thomas Elyot published *The Boke Named the Governour* in 1531.[1]

Like the *basse danse*, the pavan was a stately processional dance. According to Thoinot Arbeau's *Orchésographie* (Langres, 1588), our main source of information for the sixteenth century, 'kings, princes and great lords' used it 'to display themselves on some day of solemn festival with their fine mantles and robes of ceremony; and then the queens and the princesses and the great ladies accompany them with the long trains of their dresses let down and trailing behind them, or sometimes carried by damsels'.[2] Arbeau's simple open-ended choreography, a stylised walk, allowed the pavan to be danced to any multiple of four semibreves, or even to triple-time music with a dotted minim rather than a minim beat. Thomas Morley wrote in *A Plaine and Easie Introduction to Practical Musicke* (1597; repr. 1937) that the pavan was 'a kind of staid music ordained for grave dancing and most commonly made of three strains, whereof every strain is played or sung twice; a strain they make to contain eight, twelve, or sixteen semibreves as they list, yet fewer than eight I have not seen in any Pavan'. He added that dancers could cope with any length of strain so long as it consisted of an even number of bars: 'you must cast your music by four [semibreves], so that if you keep that rule it is no matter how many fours you put in your strain, for it will fall out well enough in the end'.[3]

The galliard

The galliard was a lively hopping and kicking dance using the *cinque pas*, a pattern of five steps danced to six minims of music. Arbeau wrote that it is called *gaillarde* 'because one must be blithe and lively to dance it'; it could be danced by one couple or several, or alternatively by a single man as a solo. To judge from the musical sources, the dance developed several decades later than the pavan, perhaps because, in Italy at least, the pavan was at first paired with the saltarello. Many early galliards were derived from pavans by translating the duple-time music into triple time, which meant that they tended to have the same structure as their parent pavans. Morley wrote that it was 'a lighter and more stirring kind of dancing than the Pavan, consisting of the same number of strains; and look how many fours of semibreves you put in the strain of your Pavan so many times six minims must you put in the strain of your Galliard'. In fact, by the time Morley wrote those words English composers had largely stopped deriving galliards from pavans, and were writing them in all shapes and sizes. A fairly constant feature, however, was an attractive rhythmic instability created by regrouping the six minims from the normal $3 + 3$ to the $2 + 2 + 2$ hemiola pattern, and by grouping crotchets $3 + 3$ instead of $2 + 2 + 2$, so that three distinct triple patterns can sometimes be heard, at the levels of crotchets, minims and semibreves.

The almand

The third type of dance in *Lachrimae*, the almand, alman or almain (*allemande* in French), seems to have originated in Germany, possibly in Nuremberg around 1540, hence its name.[4] As Morley put it, it is 'a more heavy dance then this [the galliard] (fitly representing the nature of the people whose name it carrieth) so that no extraordinary motions are used in dancing of it'. According to Arbeau, it was danced by a line of couples, like the pavan, and the basic pattern consisted of three steps and a hop. Morley wrote that 'It is made of strains, sometimes two, sometimes three, and every strain is made by [groups of] four [semibreves]', adding that the strains of 'the usual Alman containeth the time of eight [semibreves], and most commonly in short notes'; the basic pulse is usually in crotchets rather than minims. Elizabethan almands tend to be jolly four-square pieces, with catchy tunes supported by simple diatonic harmonies.

Composition, arrangement and performance

There were two main ways of writing sixteenth-century dance music. In Italy and Germany the principle of weaving florid parts against a cantus firmus did not entirely disappear with the *basse danse* and the *alta capella*. The tune is still in the tenor in the few surviving consort examples of the *Hoftanz* (a late German type of *basse danse*), as well as a number of early sixteenth-century Italian dances now in Munich.[5] The cantus firmus tradition also continued in a new form in the many Italian dances based on standard chord sequences and the bass patterns associated with them, such as the *Passamezzo antico*, the *Passamezzo moderno* and the *Romanesca*. In France and The Netherlands, by contrast, dances were usually settings of a tune in the top part, often derived from a polyphonic chanson.

In practice, the distinction between the two types is not always clear cut. Standard descants were often associated with the bass patterns; an obvious example from Tudor England is the tune 'Greensleeves', a descant to a combination of the *Passamezzo antico* and the *Romanesca*.[6] Similarly, dances with a tune in the top part often have an associated bass line, the standard way of harmonising the tune; a good example is Arbeau's pavan 'Belle qui tiens ma vie' and the dances related to it, such as the 'Allemande du Prince' and 'La Coranto', best known from Byrd's keyboard setting and a piece in Morley's *Consort Lessons*.[7] The two types became less distinct in the late sixteenth century, when original composi-tions by mainstream composers supplanted the older repertory of dances based on popular tunes and chord sequences. The various set-tings for consort and solo instruments of popular English pavans, such as 'Lachrimae' or the one by Peter Philips dated 1580 in the Fitzwilliam Virginal Book, usually have a common 'gist' consisting of the tune, the bass, the implied harmonies in between, and any particularly striking contrapuntal or decorative features in the inner parts.[8]

Renaissance dance music divides into two main types: the consort set-tings in four, five and six parts, and the versions for solo instruments such as the keyboard, the lute and the cittern. The consort settings were pre-sumably composed and arranged mostly for the professional groups that accompanied dancing, though some survive in prints or manuscripts pub-lished or copied partly with amateurs in mind. Dance musicians usually performed from memory, which is presumably why most of the manu-scripts they owned or used have disappeared; a rare exception is the collec-tion of consort dances in the Arundel or Lumley part-books, apparently copied by dance musicians in England around 1560.[9] Since most six-teenth-century amateurs came to music by way of solo instruments such as the lute or the virginals, it is not surprising that much more sixteenth-century dance music survives in solo settings than in consort versions.

One of the main differences between the two repertories is that dances set for solo instruments were usually provided with written-out orna-mentation, while most of the consort settings are plain. There are three reasons for this. Plucked instruments need ornamentation to prolong the sound, and the nature of tablature, which tells the player where to put his fingers rather than what notes to play, makes it difficult for the less experienced player to improvise ornamentation. Also, professionals had no need for written-out ornamentation, for much of their training consisted of learning how to improvise florid ornamentation.[10] Thus the difference between the two types is greater on the page than it would have been in performance. Some sources with tablature parts, such as the collection of lute trios by Giovanni Pacolini or Pacoloni published in 1564, or Matthew Holmes's mixed consort books in GB-Cu, have elaborate written-out divisions that give a vivid impression of how professional groups would have elaborated dance music in performance.[11]

The Elizabethan dance repertory

The few English dances that survive from before Elizabeth's reign suggest that the repertory was largely imported: three of the six consort dances preserved in keyboard reduction in the mid-century GB-Lbl, Royal Appendix MS 58 are related to pieces in contemporary continental publications.[12] However, the dances in the Arundel part-books show that a distinctively English repertory was beginning to emerge around 1560. One feature is the emphasis on five-part writing: the compilers apparently made an effort to collect five-part dances, and to convert existing four-part pieces into five by adding a specially written Quintus part. So far as we can tell from the rather scattered and fragmentary sources, five-part writing remained the norm for dance music throughout Elizabeth's reign. By contrast, four-part writing remained the standard in Italy and much of northern Europe until the late sixteenth century, and in Germany a sizeable body of five-part dance music only developed around 1600 as English expatriates such as William Brade and Thomas Simpson disseminated their native idiom.

The most distinctive feature of Elizabethan dance music is the prominence given to pavans or pavan-galliard pairs. Nearly a third of the fifty-odd dances in the Arundel part-books are pavans, a much higher proportion than in equivalent continental collections. Of the three books of *danseries* published by Jean d'Estrée in Paris in 1559, for instance, two consist entirely of branles while the third contains only four pavans in a varied selection of forty-five dances, including branles, allemandes, galliards and *basse danses*.[13] If anything, the proportion of pavans increases in later Elizabethan collections. The sequence of twenty-five five-part dances by Peter Philips and others in one of the score-books supposedly copied by Francis Tregian (1574–1619), includes six pavan-galliard pairs and four separate pavans.[14] Holborne's *Pavans, Galliards, Almains* consists of twenty-seven pavan-galliard pairs, six almands and five corants. The fifty-three pavans in D-Kl, 4° MS mus. 125, 1–5, were drawn partly or possibly exclusively from the English repertory (see Chapter 2).

The fashion for pairing pavans and galliards declined in late Elizabethan England. Although there are some notable exceptions, such as the paired keyboard pavans and galliards by Byrd in My Ladye Nevells Booke of 1591 or those in Rosseter's *Lessons for Consort*,[15] English composers around 1600 increasingly preferred to write separate pavans and galliards. Even when they were paired in collections, as in *Pavans, Galliards, Almains*, they were often not thematically related, and *Lachrimae* is remarkable for its lack of pairs, as we shall see. Many of the most influential English works, such as Philips's 1580 Pavan and 'Lachrimae', were apparently written as singletons, though galliards were sometimes provided for them by others, particularly by composers working in the Anglo-German repertory.[16]

Little need be said about the Elizabethan almand, except to note that the dance seems to have gone through a period of neglect in the 1580s and 90s, only to enjoy a revival soon after 1600, perhaps because of the sudden popularity of the almand-like dances written for Jacobean masques. The change was quite sudden: of two comparable sequences of consort dance music in manuscripts apparently compiled by court wind players, one, US-NH, Filmer MS 2 (*c.* 1600), includes only two almands with six pavans and thirteen galliards, while the Jacobean layer of GB-Cfm, Mus. MS 734 (*c.* 1615), includes a single pavan in a sequence of twenty-three almands, including several written for masques.[17] By contrast, pavans and galliards continued to dominate the Anglo-German repertory for several decades.

The late Elizabethan pavan

The pavan came to dominate the Elizabethan dance repertory at a time when it was in decline in some parts of Europe; if the Italian dance manuals are anything to go by, it was more or less obsolete there by 1600.[18] But this does not necessarily mean that the English continued to dance the pavan long after other nations, for there are signs even in the Arundel part-books that it had begun to make the transition from functional dance to abstract musical genre. Since Morley advised composers to keep to strains of even numbers of breves so that their pavans could be danced to, the presence of a strain of five breves in a pavan in the Arundel part-books suggests it was not written for dancing. The pavan's galliard is ascribed to 'Innocents' – presumably the Innocent of Cremona who joined the English court violin consort in 1550.[19]

Pavans with strains of uneven numbers of breves become much more common in later Elizabethan sources. There is one with a five-breve strain in the Dublin Virginal Book (*c.* 1570), and a beautiful one by Joseph Lupo based on Lassus's chanson 'Susanne un jour' with a second strain of eight-and-a-half breves; it was probably written soon after 1570, when the chanson was published in London.[20] By the end of the century irregular strains had become almost routine: nine of the twenty-seven pavans in Holborne's *Pavans, Galliards, Almains* have them, as do twenty-six of the fifty-three pavans in Kassel MS 125; only three of the ten pavans in *Lachrimae* have regular strains. The most extreme type of irregularity encountered in pavans is when the last strain turns wholly or partially into triple time. Morley's 'Sacred End Pavan' (so called because it ends with an idea used in several anthems, see Chapter 4) is the best-known example.[21] It has a brief triple-time section in the last strain, and was probably the model for a number of pavans with triple-time passages in the Anglo-German repertory.

Most English pavans written around 1600 seem about as far removed from the dance floor as the examples by Fauré and Ravel, and this not just because of their irregular strains. As early as the Arundel part-books there are a few pieces – such as a group of three canonic pavans and one scored for five bass instruments[22] – that seem designed to be listened to rather than danced to, and the genre increased steadily in complexity and musical interest during Elizabeth's reign. Early Elizabethan pavans sometimes have strains of four breves, or eight-breve strains divided into two four-breve phrases with matching openings leading to contrasted cadences, as in the first strain of a keyboard pavan by 'Mr Marchant'.[23] A slightly more sophisticated variant of this pattern is the eight-breve strain that divides into two four-breve contrasted phrases, as in the first strain of a pavan by Augustine Bassano copied by Francis Tregian.[24] Later composers such as Philips or Holborne had no trouble writing continuous strains of eight or more breves, though some of the simpler (and earlier?) ones in *Pavans, Galliards, Almains* still cadence on the first beat of the fourth or fifth breve of an eight-breve strain while maintaining melodic or contrapuntal momentum; good examples are the first strain of no. 3, the second of no. 7, the first of no. 15, all three of no. 37, the third of no. 47, and the first and third of no. 51, 'Posthuma'. Dowland used the device in all three strains of 'Lachrimae'.

In the 1580s and 90s English pavans became increasingly complex and contrapuntal, and composers began to develop special effects or 'topics' in their third strains. Sometimes ideas were borrowed from other genres, as in Morley's 'Sacred End Pavan', but more often the models were other pavans, so that a web of subtle connections developed. One of the most influential pieces was Peter Philips's 1580 Pavan, which has an apparently invented plainsong-like cantus firmus in the Cantus accompanied by patterns of three repeated notes. Philips probably got the idea from Nicholas Strogers's fine 'In Nomine Pavan', so called because its third strain borrows a three-note accompaniment pattern (but not, oddly, the cantus firmus) from a popular In Nomine by Robert Parsons.[25] In turn, Philips's 1580 Pavan influenced many later works, such as 'Southerne's Pavan' by Morley, Holborne's 'Decrevi', *Pavans, Galliards, Almains*, no. 35, and a number of pieces in the Anglo-German repertory, including four in D-Kl, 4° MS mus. 125, 1–5.[26] Peter Philips also seems to have started a fashion for chromatic passages with his 'Dolorosa Pavan' of 1593, though a popular piece by Thomas Tomkins proved even more influential.[27] 'Lachrimae' was at the centre of this tradition, and we shall see in Chapter 4 how Dowland developed it to an unprecedented degree in the 'passionate pavans'.

Tonality

There has been a recent tendency to try to explain the tonality of all types of Renaissance music in terms of modal theory, but it is not clear that the composers of Elizabethan dance music thought in those terms. Morley explained the modes in some detail in the annotations to the third part of

A Plaine and Easie Introduction, but gave the impression in the main text that they were obsolete, describing the 'Eight Tunes' or psalm tones used by 'the churchmen for keeping their keys' merely as 'some shadow of the ancient "modi" whereof Boethius and Glareanus have written so much'.[28] Similarly, Thomas Campion paid lip-service to the modes in the section on 'the Tones of Musicke' in his *New Way of Making Fowre Parts in Counter-point* (?1613–14), though he stated that 'the Key, or Moode, or Tone . . . all signifie the same thing'.[29]

A 'Table of Tones', set down around 1620 in a manuscript of John Bull's keyboard music in Vienna, shows that the twelve church modes as codified by Glareanus in his *Dodecachordon* (Basle, 1547) had been reduced to eight.[30] The first four are effectively minor keys, D minor (1), G minor (2), A minor (3) and E minor (4), while the others are major keys, C major (5), F major (6), D major (7) and G major (8). The system of authentic and plagal modes has been abandoned, and Tones 2 and 6 have a B flat key signature. Elizabethan dance music inhabits the same tonal landscape, though had the list been compiled in England it might have included C minor and B flat major rather than E minor and D major, which only became common in English consort music in the 1620s and 30s. Composers increasingly exploited the full range of stringed instruments, stepping outside the *ambitus* or range of the mode, and the tone is defined as much by the accidentals used as by the 'final' or concluding note. Tone 1 (D minor) normally ranges between B flat and G sharp, Tone 2 (G minor) between E flat and C sharp, Tone 3 (A minor) between B flat and G sharp, and so on.

Morley was at a loss when he tried to explain modulation, a concept foreign to the modal system. His Philomathes asks whether there is a 'general rule to be given for an instruction for keeping of the key', but the Master replies 'No, for it must proceed only of the judgement of the composer', and Morley could only use the terminology of the hexachord system to discuss modulation: 'though the air of every key be different one from the other yet some love (by a wonder of nature) to be joined to others, so that if you begin your song in Gam ut you may conclude it either in C fa ut or D sol re and from thence come again to Gam ut; likewise if you begin your song in D sol re you may end in A re and come again to D sol re, etc.' Campion was much more specific, and described possible modulations to (in modern terms) the dominant and the relative major of

G minor and A minor, Tones 1 and 3. In Tone 8, G major (which of course has no relative major), Campion suggests closes in A minor, the supertonic, or C major, the subdominant. Charles Butler recognised the dominant and the relative major as 'Secundari Cadences', but thought those on the second, sixth and seventh degrees of the scale 'Improper Cadences', 'strange and informal to the Air' and 'sparingly to bee used'.[31]

It is striking that the harmonic idiom of English dance music did not become noticeably more modern during Elizabeth's reign; the modern traits are present in the pavans of the early Elizabethan Arundel part-books just as strongly as those by Holborne and Dowland. I believe this is because of the influence of Italian chord sequences such as the *Passamezzo antico* (usually I–VII–I–V / I–VII–I–V–I in Tone 2), the *Passamezzo moderno* (usually I–IV–I–V / I–IV–I–V–I in Tone 8), the *Romanesca* (usually III–VII–I–V / III–VII–I–V–I in Tone 2), and the *Bergamasca* (usually I–IV–V–I in Tone 5), which showed mid-century English composers how to organise their dance music using patterns of logical progressions punctuated by regular cadences.

Most English settings of Italian chord sequences are in the lute and keyboard repertories, where composers could draw on established idioms of written-out variations to elaborate them at some length. But their influence can also be heard in many early consort pavans. A five-part piece in the Arundel part-books[32] is a mixture of *Passamezzo antico* and *Romanesca* patterns, while the pavan by 'Master Tayler' in the Dublin Virginal Book begins as an elaboration of the *Bergamasca* and hardly departs from the 'three-chord trick'. Not surprisingly, the influence of Italian chord sequences became diluted later, though they still seem to govern the outline progressions of many more harmonically complex pavans. Taking the chords that begin and end strains, five Tone 2 pavans by Holborne in *Pavans, Galliards, Almains*, nos. 1, 23, 25, 31 and 33 outline I–I / V–V / III–I, while the two-strain Tone 8 pavan no. 3 outlines I–I / VII–I, a pattern developed in no. 41 as I–I / VII–V / I–I. Similar things can be found in *Lachrimae*: 'Gementes' outlines I–I / VII–V / V–I, 'Unton' outlines I–I / V–V / III–I, while the pattern used in 'Tristes', Coactae' and 'Amantis', I–I / II–V / V–I, recalls the 'strange and informal' modulations to the supertonic advocated by Campion. Striking juxtapositions such as I–VII and V–III in these English pavans surely owe more to Italian chord sequences than to modal thinking.

4

The seven 'Passionate Pavans'

The seven pavans that begin *Lachrimae* are among the best-known and best-loved pieces of instrumental music written before the eighteenth century. Their serene beauty speaks for itself, yet they also raise many questions. Why are there seven of them? How are they related? Do they contain ideas borrowed from other composers? Were they intended to be performed as a cycle? What is the significance of the Latin titles? Do they have any bearing on their musical character? How does the cycle exemplify the Elizabethan cult of melancholy?

'Lachrimae Antiquae'

Any attempt to answer these questions must begin with 'Antiquae', the 'Old Tears'. As its title indicates, it was not new when *Lachrimae* appeared. It was perhaps the single most popular and widely distributed instrumental piece of the period: it occurs in about a hundred manuscripts and prints from England, Scotland, The Netherlands, France, Germany, Austria, Denmark, Sweden and Italy, in settings for lute solo, lute duet, lute trio with two viols, cittern, bandora, recorder, violin, division viol, lyra viol, keyboard, mixed consort, and four- and five-part viols or violins, as well as a number of song versions.[1]

The sources suggest that the earliest 'Lachrimae' was for solo lute. Of the eighteen copies in English lute books, one was printed by William Barley in his *New Booke of Tabliture* (1596), and a number of others come from manuscripts that apparently date from before 1604. One of the earliest was copied by Matthew Holmes into GB-Cu, Dd. 2.11, f. 81, in the early 1590s, and was originally intended for a six-course lute – which suggests it is a relatively early work.[2] By contrast, the earliest source of the famous lute-song setting, 'Flow my teares', seems to be *The Second*

Booke of Songs or Ayres, published in 1600. The song is almost certainly an adaptation of the pavan rather than the other way round, for Dowland headed it 'Lacrime' as if it was a version of a well-known piece, and the poem has no metrical regularity: it shows signs of having been written to fit the tune.[3] Dowland seems to have arranged a number of his songs from instrumental dances (see Chapter 5), and in general the type of lute song he popularised had its roots in the English broadside ballad, and had connections with the Italian *villanella* and the French *voix de ville* – genres that involved adding words to existing popular tunes.

The settings of 'Lachrimae' divide by key into three groups, G minor, A minor and D minor. Diana Poulton argued that G minor was Dowland's original choice, since it is the key of the copy in Dd.2.11, f. 81, and most of those in lute sources, and it is a good key for the lute. She suggested that A minor, a less idiomatic lute key, was subsequently chosen for the benefit of the singers in 'Flow my teares' and the stringed instruments in 'Antiquae'.[4] But the situation is not that simple. Matthew Holmes copied a fine but little-known A minor setting into Dd.2.11, ff. 75^v–77, a few pages earlier than the G minor one, while there is another A minor version without divisions in GB-Lbl, MS Hirsch M.1353, f. 11^v (*c.* 1595). Moreover, I have argued that the five-part A minor setting in Kassel 4° MS mus. 125, 1–5, no. 42, is a pre-publication version of 'Antiquae', a souvenir of one of Dowland's visits to the town in the 1590s.[5] To complicate things further, the earliest datable continental lute setting, 'Pavana a 5 voc. Dulandi Angli', no. 91 in *Flores musicae* ii (Heidelberg, 1600) by the Leipzig lutenist Johann Rude, is in G minor, and its title could be taken to mean that it is an arrangement from a five-part consort setting in that key.

All this goes to show that we are wrong to look for a 'definitive' or 'original' version of 'Lachrimae', as we might do for a piece by Bach or Chopin. Dowland and his contemporaries would have played their own pieces in a semi-improvised manner from a memorised 'gist', much as jazz musicians do today. Each time they wrote them down they doubtless would have felt free to vary the details, to suit particular circumstances, intended recipients, or just changing fashion. This explains why popular pieces often circulated in a number of variant versions, and it also suggests that 'Antiquae' is an independent working from the common 'Lachrimae' gist rather than an arrangement dependent on some 'original' lute setting.

What, then, is the gist of 'Lachrimae'? The Tone 3 pavan consists of three strains of eight, eight and eight-and-a-half breves, divided internally by cadences at bb. 5, 12 and 20, outlining the conventional harmonic pattern I–I–I / III–IV–V / V–V–I. What was new about the piece, and what probably ensured its popularity, was the concise richness of its melodic and motivic writing. Earlier composers tended to make do with one or two distinctive ideas per strain, padding them out with rather featureless and uncoordinated free contrapuntal writing. By contrast, in 'Lachrimae' the listener is immediately struck by the number of meaningful ideas, and gradually becomes aware that they are tightly and economically controlled; most of them are related, and there is little padding, even in the inner parts of 'Antiquae'. That is why an unusual amount of detail from the inner parts was preserved in the gist transmitted in later arrangements, such as the keyboard settings by Sweelinck and his followers.

In fact, an extraordinary amount of the material of 'Antiquae' (from now on my analysis refers specifically to the five-part setting in *Lachrimae*) derives in some way from the famous four-note motif $a'–g'–f'–e'$ that begins the Cantus, a musical emblem of falling tears. This tear motif, as I shall call it, is answered by another, $c''–b'–a'–g\sharp'$, a third higher. As Lionel Pike has pointed out, there are falling or rising fourths outlined in every bar of the Cantus except 12–14, and they also occur regularly in the Bassus, particularly in the first and third strains.[6] Thirds are also constantly used, either rising, as in the brief contrapuntal passage in b. 3 or the declamatory passage in bb. 12–14, or falling, as in the sequential sighing motif in b. 5 of the Cantus, echoed in such places as bb. 5–6 of the bass, b. 10 of the Quintus, or the contrapuntal idea in bb. 11–12. Furthermore, the fourths and the thirds are cunningly related by the plaintive minor sixth that links the two tetrachords at the beginning of the Cantus. The ear also notices that it is reflected in the simultaneous minor sixths in the Quintus and the Bassus, and that the Bassus also outlines the descending tetrachord, allowing for an octave transposition and the omission of the second note, G. Two other significant details need to be mentioned at this stage: the figure (a) that rises by step at different speeds at the opening of the Altus and Tenor, and the falling fifth in quavers (b) in the middle of b. 3 of the Altus (see Ex. 4.1).

Ex. 4.1 'Antiquae', bb. 1–8 (lute part omitted)

The tetrachord also colours the tonality of 'Lachrimae'. The pavan is formally in Tone 3, equivalent to A minor, but one can also hear the influence of Tone 4, effectively the phrygian mode on E, making it similar to the hypoaeolian tenth mode as described by Glareanus and Zarlino.[7] The tone–tone–semitone pattern of the falling tetrachord was exploited in the Renaissance for its affective power; indeed, the phrygian mode is made up of two such tetrachords, E–D–C–B and A–G–F–E. When A–G–F–E occurs in the Bassus, as it does repeatedly in the first and third strains, it makes the characteristic phrygian cadence of the Baroque period. As often happens in English pavans, the tonality changes abruptly at the beginning of the second strain: the music starts in C major and touches D minor before settling again on to a phrygian cadence on E. The phrygian colour returns in the third strain: it starts with two bars of dominant pedal on E, returns to an E major chord in b. 20, and is then taken up with a contrapuntal point that features the expressive four-note figure E–B–C–B. Note also how Dowland achieves a sense of climax by pushing the top note of the Cantus up a step in each strain, from c″, to d″, and finally to e″.

The tear motif

Several writers have claimed to find models for the tear motif. Otto Mies and Diana Poulton respectively suggested Créquillon's chanson 'Cessez mes yeulx' and Cauleray's 'En esperant'.[8] But the semitone falls in the wrong place in the former, and occurs unobtrusively in the middle of a phrase of the latter. More promisingly, Rudolf Henning suggested Rore's madrigal 'Quando lieto sperai', which sets a slightly elaborated tetrachord to the words 'lagrime dunque'.[9] John Ward questioned the need to search for a model, but offered the opening of 'Smith's Pavan' (actually 'pavana Bryches'), a single-line division part in the Arundel part-books, as well as the observation that 'the tones *a g f e* also form the basis of most *Romanesca* discants'.[10]

The problem with this line of enquiry is that, by itself, the falling tetrachord is a commonplace, a standard emblem of grief. Lionel Pike has drawn attention to its occurrences in madrigals by Giovanni Gabrieli, Marenzio, Wert, Monteverdi and others, as well as Josquin's 'Mille regrets' and Victoria's 1572 setting of 'O vos omnes', and it is familiar as the standard form of the *Passacaglia* ground bass, which became associated with laments in the 1620s and 30s.[11] Its chromatic form was also developed as a grief emblem in ascending as well as descending forms, notably in Dowland's 'Forlorn Hope' and 'Farewell' fantasias.[12]

Clearly, to establish a credible connection between 'Lachrimae' and earlier compositions we need more than four notes in common. In fact, there are two works probably known to Dowland that use the complete tear motif – the two tetrachords connected by the minor sixth. David Pinto has drawn attention to Lassus's setting of the words 'Laboravi in gemitu meo' in 'Domine ne in furore tuo', the first of his *Psalmi Davidis poenitentiales* (Munich, 1584) (see Ex. 4.2).[13] Like 'Lachrimae', the passage is in Tone 3 with phrygian leanings, and sets a highly relevant text: 'I am weary with my groaning; all the night long I make my bed to swim; I water my couch with tears'. There is no direct evidence that Dowland knew Lassus's cycle, though there is another connection between 'Lachrimae' and the Seven Penitential Psalms, as we shall see.

Ex. 4.2 O. Lassus, 'Laboravi in gemitu meo', bb. 1–4, from 'Domine ne in furore tuo'

Dowland would certainly have known the other work, 'Parto da voi, mio sole' from Marenzio's third book of six-part madrigals (Venice, 1585), for it was reprinted as 'Now I must part' in *Musica transalpina* (1588), and it has been suggested that the original Italian text was the inspiration for the text of Dowland's song 'Now, O now I needs must part' from *The First Booke*.[14] We should not be surprised that Dowland looked to Marenzio for inspiration. He travelled to Italy in 1595 to study with the Italian and extolled his virtues in *The First Booke*, even printing a rather inconsequential letter from him, 'not thinking it any disgrace to be proud of the judgement of so excellent a man'. Furthermore, he based part of his song 'Would my conceit that first enforced my woe' from *The First Booke* on Marenzio's 'Ahi, dispietata morte'.[15]

'Parto da voi, mio sole', also in Tone 3, contains the complete tear motif using the same pitches and virtually the same rhythms, though it is in the Altus rather than the Cantus, and the last note is a G natural rather than G sharp. What makes the passage more significant is that the tear motif is accompanied by rising figures in the Cantus and the Sextus similar to (a) at the beginning of Dowland's Altus and Tenor (see Ex. 4.3). Another madrigal by Marenzio, the five-part 'Rivi, fontane, e fiumi' from the anthology *Le gioie musicali* (Venice, 1589), also begins with a rising idea similar to (a) accompanying a version of the tear motif in paired imitation that is strikingly similar to the opening of 'Verae'.[16] Dowland used this contrapuntal version of the motif in the third strain

Ex. 4.3 L. Marenzio, 'Parto da voi, mio sole', bb. 1–3

Ex. 4.4 L. Marenzio, 'Rivi, fontane, e fiumi', bb. 1–3

of 'Tristes' and the opening of 'Amantis'. Note also the falling quavers in the Tenor, b. 2, similar to (b) in 'Antiquae' (see Ex. 4.4). Of course, we have no means of knowing how conscious any of these borrowings were, though at the very least they suggest that Dowland was immersed in the music of his great continental contemporaries.

Musical rhetoric

Why was Dowland attracted to Marenzio? At first sight it is strange that a famous lutenist at the height of his powers should want to travel to Italy to study with a madrigal composer – a genre to which he never contributed, so far as we know. Dowland was doubtless caught up by the enthusiasm for the Italian madrigal in Elizabethan England. Marenzio, the most famous madrigalist of his generation, was particularly venerated in England. He dominated the printed anthologies – Thomas Watson's *Italian Madrigals Englished* (1590) consists almost entirely of his works – and was praised by Morley and Henry Peacham, Dowland's friend and neighbour.[17] Peacham wrote in *The Compleat Gentleman* (1622; repr. 1968) that Marenzio was 'a little and blacke man' who excelled everyone 'for delicious Aire and sweet Invention in Madrigals'; he listed works 'the Muses themselves might not have been ashamed to have had composed'.

But Marenzio's madrigals also exemplified techniques that could be applied to other genres. We are familiar with the techniques of literal word-painting associated with the madrigal. As Morley put it, 'you must have a care that when your matter signifieth "ascending", "high", "heaven", and such like you make your music ascend; and by the contrary where your ditty speaketh of "descending", "lowness", "depth", "hell", and others such, you must make your music descend'. He also wrote about more subtle ways in which harmony can be made to express emotion. One of his examples is virtually a description of 'Lachrimae': 'when you would express a lamentable passion, then must you use motions proceeding by half notes, flat thirds, and flat sixths, which of their nature are sweet, specially being taken in the true tune and natural air with discretion and judgement'.[18]

Unfortunately, Morley ignored the most important element of the Italian style: the use of rhetorical figures to create a musical language of heightened and focused emotional intensity. As Robin Headlam Wells has pointed out, in the absence of formal academies in England, the Elizabethans looked to books on rhetoric to disseminate humanist ideas.[19] Several contemporary writers pointed out that the standard rhetorical devices used to heighten emotion in literature had musical counterparts. Francis Bacon wrote in *Sylva sylvarum* (1627) that 'There be in Musick certaine Figures, or Tropes; almost agreeing with the Figures of Rhetorike; And with the Affections of the Minde, and other Senses'. Henry Peacham made the same point at greater length: 'Yea in my opinion, no Rhetorique more perswadeth, or hath greater power over the mind; nay, hath not Musicke her figures, the same which Rhetorique? What is a Revert [contrary motion] but her Antistrophe? her reports [imitation], but sweete Anaphora's? her counterchange of points, Antimetabole's?

her passionate Aires, but Prosopopoeas? with infinite other of the same nature'.[20]

These rhetorical figures have recently been studied by writers concerned with the performance of English lute songs.[21] While some apply directly to speaking and (by extension) singing, others were formulated for literary composition, and can in some cases be extended to musical composition – and to music that does not depend on words. The second and third strains of 'Antiquae' illustrate the point. As Peacham recognised, imitative counterpoint was one of the most important rhetorical devices available to the composer, since the technique of imitation involved matching an appropriate musical figure to each phrase of a text, and the constant repetition of figures was the musical equivalent of *anaphora*, or the sententious figures of repetition in poetry. Counterpoint was all-pervasive in polyphonic vocal music, but tightly organised, imitative, 'rhetorical' counterpoint was relatively rare in dance music before Dowland, at least among lutenist composers.

The second strain of 'Antiquae' contains three imitative points, corresponding to the phrases 'since pittie is fled' (c), 'and teares, and sighes, and groanes' (d) and 'my wearie dayes' (e) in the third verse of 'Flow my teares'. But Dowland ensures the continuity necessary in a pavan partly by extending (c) over the internal cadence on the first beat at b. 12, and partly by relating the three ideas to each other: (c) is mostly concerned with falling thirds, which are converted into rising thirds in (d) and decorated in (e) (see Ex. 4.5). Such relationships are more common in instrumental music than vocal music because composers did not have to produce appropriately contrasted material for each phrase of the text. As Morley put it in his description of the fantasia: 'in this may more art be shown than in any other music because the composer is tied to nothing, but that he may add, diminish, and alter at his pleasure'.

The basic rhetorical device exemplified by (d) is *auxesis*. Henry Peacham senior (the father of Dowland's friend) described it in *The Garden of Eloquence* (1577) as 'when we make our saying grow and increase by an orderly placing of our words, making the latter word always exceed the former, in force of signifycation'. Its musical equivalent, the repetition of figures in an ascending sequence, is variously called *gradatio*, *climax* or *anabasis*.[22] It was recognised that the intensification of emotion produced by *auxesis* or *gradatio* was made more effective by preparing it with a

Ex. 4.5 'Antiquae', bb. 9–16 (lute part omitted)

descent, in subject matter, style of delivery or musical pitch – illustrated by (c). As John Hoskins wrote (1599), '[To] make the matter seeme the higher advaunced, sometimes [the figure] descends the lower . . . it is an ornament of speech, to begin att the lowest that you the better aspire to the height of amplyficacion'.[23] The problem with (d) in 'Flow my teares' is that it is set to words – 'and teares, and sighes, and grones' or 'and feare, and griefe, and paine' – that seem to call for a falling, reflective figure rather than a confident, rising figure and the increase of volume associated with such figures. According to Michel Le Faucheur (1657), ''Tis manifest that the Voyce must be rais'd accordingly by the same degrees of elevation to answer every step of the Figure, till it is at the utmost height of it', while Athanasius Kircher wrote (1650) that *anabasis* or *ascensio* 'is a musical passage through which we express exalted, rising, or elevated and eminent thoughts'.[24] More evidence, perhaps, that 'Lachrimae' was originally an instrumental pavan.

The third strain of 'Antiquae' has two rhetorical ideas. One is harmonic rather than melodic: the recurring g♮–g♯ false relations are

Ex. 4.6 'Antiquae', bb. 20–5 (lute part omitted)

examples of *parrhesia*, the use of pungent language to reprehend the hearers for some fault, according to the anonymous author of *Rhetorica ad Herennium*.[25] The other is the contrapuntal point (f) that takes up its second half, from b. 20. It is a good example of *ecphonesis* or *exclamatio*, one of the 'sharp figures' that Henry Peacham senior thought suitable for stirring up vehement emotions:

> when through affection either of anger, sorrow, gladnesse, marveyling, feare, or any such lyke, we break out in voyce with an exclamation, & outcry to expresse the passions of our minde, after this manner. O lamentable estate, O cursed misery, O wicked impudency, O joy imcomparable, O rare and singuler bewty.[26]

Dowland and his contemporaries usually set expletives of this sort to figures that begin with a syncopated long note followed by shorter notes, as (f) does (see Ex. 4.6). Dowland set it to the phrase 'Happie, happie they that in hell', which is not the best rhetorical match for the music, since it draws attention to the word 'happy' to the detriment of the meaning of the phrase as a whole. This is another hint that the words of 'Flow my teares' were added to 'Lachrimae'; we shall see in a moment that the figure (f) is connected with sacred rather than secular words.

The nature of the cycle

We do not know when Dowland had the idea of creating seven pavans out of 'Antiquae', though 'Antiquae Novae', 'Gementes', 'Tristes', 'Coactae',

'Amantis' and 'Verae' may have been written especially for *Lachrimae*: none of them exists in lute settings, and only 'Antiquae Novae' is found in any other contemporary source – Thomas Simpson published his own five-part arrangement in 1610.[27] It is not always appreciated today how novel the concept of a sequence of seven related pavans was. Of course, the technique of creating one dance out of another was fundamental to Renaissance dance music: galliards were routinely modelled on pavans, *tordions* on *basse danses* and so on, and soon after 1600 German composers began to publish suite-like sequences of dances with some related movements. But only Dowland thought of writing a variation cycle using a single type of dance rather than a selection of the dances of the day, and he was the first composer to use dance forms and variation techniques to explore the elevated areas of feeling hitherto exclusively associated with contrapuntal genres such as the motet or the fantasia.

Why seven pavans? The number seven was thought to be numerologically significant, and Lionel Pike has also suggested that Dowland chose it partly because it combines four and three, the intervals that dominate 'Lachrimae'.[28] But there are also obvious parallels with other seven-fold cycles, such as the Seven Last Words of Jesus on the Cross, the Seven Sorrows of Mary, the Seven Deadly Sins, and the Seven Penitential Psalms. We have seen that Dowland may have found the tear motif in a passage from Lassus's setting of the Penitential Psalms, and he would certainly have known William Hunnis's *Seven Sobs of a Sorrowfull Soule for Sinne* (1581), a collection of devotional verse including 'those seven Psalmes of the Princelie Prophet of David, commonlie called Pœnitentiall: framed into a forme of familiar praiers, and reduced into meeter'. It was enduringly popular: ten reprints are known between 1583 and 1629.[29]

There is an unexpected if tortuous connection between Hunnis's *Seven Sobs of a Sorrowfull Soule for Sinne* and 'Lachrimae'. Two anthems, Morley's 'O Jesu meeke' and Thomas Weelkes's 'Give ear, O Lord', are settings of lines from a section of the book entitled 'A Handfull of Honiesuckles'. The two anthems are also related to each other and to Christopher Tye's anthem 'I lift my heart to thee' (a setting of Psalm 25, v. 1) by the fact that they have essentially the same refrain, 'Mercie, good Lord, mercie' or 'have mercie now on mee', set to passages of counterpoint using the same figure (f) that Dowland used in 'Lachrimae' (see Ex. 4.6).[30] This idea appears at the end of Morley's 'Sacred End' pavan, hence its name, and is also the subject of Daniel Farrant's 'Four-Note' pavan, which in turn seems to be a pair with Alfonso Ferrabosco II's 'Four-Note' pavan, based on a different four-note figure.[31] Like 'Lachrimae', Ferrabosco's pavan was used as a song, Ben Jonson's 'Hymn to God the Father', 'Hear me, O God'. Thus, while it is not clear exactly what the significance of these relationships is, they certainly suggest that the 'Sacred End' figure, as I shall call it, has some sort of religious significance.

In this connection, it is interesting that Dowland gave his pavan the title 'Lachrimae', 'tears', and the cycle the subtitle 'seaven teares'. In Elizabethan literature tears were normally expected from women, children and old men, and were associated with moderate emotion. As Marjory E. Lange puts it, 'a person does not weep for minor sorrow; and in extraordinary anguish, one is more apt to throw up, or void'.[32] But in some circumstances it was acceptable for men to weep in a religious situation. Indeed, their tears could be thought of as an emblem of their status as a penitent before God, as John Donne put it: 'Powre new seas in mine eyes, so that I might / Drowne my world with my weeping earnestly, / Or wash it, if it must be drown'd no more'.[33] There were biblical precedents: David wept for his son Absalom, Peter wept over his betrayal of Jesus, and, of course, Jesus wept for Lazarus.[34] There is no reason to think that 'Lachrimae' is specifically a portrait of female tears, so it is likely that the pavan had some religious significance for Dowland, as the connections with the Penitential Psalms imply.

How can this help us understand the significance of the Latin titles? They have baffled most scholars. Peter Warlock wrote that 'it cannot be said that they go very far in the direction of illustrating the different adjectives bestowed on them', while Ernst Meyer, Diana Poulton and Warwick Edwards avoided any discussion of their meaning.[35] However, in an article concerned with esoteric readings of Dowland's songs, Anthony Rooley wrote that they 'can be seen as a Hermetic cycle describing the fall and rise of the journeying soul', and added: 'Fortunately his epigrammatic Latin titles provide the key to his intentions in these pavans; without them we would have been left forever in the dark'. But he did not enlighten his readers further, and his attempt to connect Dowland and his music to occult Neoplatonist philosophy is controversial, to say the least.[36]

Recently, David Pinto has proposed an orthodox religious interpretation of the Latin titles, taking his cue from the connection between 'Antiquae' and the Lassus Penitential Psalm.[37] He suggests that the tears are those of the penitent, starting with those caused by original sin ('Antiquae'), and the subsequent sins of fallen mankind ('Antiquae Novae'). His woes ('Gementes') and grief ('Tristes') force him into apostasy ('Coactae'). But his penitent soul wakes to the love of God ('Amantis'), and is redeemed by divine compassion ('Verae'). This is an attractive idea, not least because it helps to explain the enigmatic oxymoronic title 'Antiquae Novae', the 'new old tears'. He suggests that it refers to St Augustine's famous phrase 'pulchritudo tam antiqua et tam nova' ('O thou Beauty both so ancient and so fresh'), a reference to the 'old yet new' beauty of God, the implication being that the 'old-new' tears represent the renewal of original sin in every fallen mortal.[38] His proposal also has an interesting autobiographical dimension: he implies that the penitent is Dowland himself, and that 'Coactae' (literally 'enforced tears') is concerned with his moment of apostasy from his Catholic faith in the 1595 letter to Cecil.

But there are several problems with this exclusively religious interpretation. One is that it presupposes Dowland was still a Catholic in 1603–4: Pinto suggests that he dedicated *Lachrimae* to Queen Anne as a fellow Catholic sympathiser who could offer him protection. Dowland certainly admitted to Cecil that he had flirted with Catholicism in his youth: when he was in Paris around 1580 he 'fell aquainted' with some English Catholics who 'thrust many Idle toies into my hed of Relygion', and 'being but yonge their faire wordes overecht me & I beleved w(i)t(h) them'. But he must have subscribed to the Thirty-Nine Articles when he received his B.Mus. degree at Christ Church, Oxford on 8 July 1588, and there is no reason to doubt his unequivocal statement of allegiance later in the letter to Cecil:

> god he knoweth I never loved treason nor trechery nor never knew of any, nor never heard any mass in englande, wh(i)ch I finde is great abuse of the peple for on my soule I understande it not, wherefor I hav reformed my self to lyve acording to her ma(jes)ties lawes as I was borne under her highnes.[39]

Furthermore, although Pinto makes a good case for a connection between the Lassus Penitential Psalm and 'Antiquae', there do not seem to be any connections between other motets in Lassus's cycle and the rest of the 'Lachrimae' pavans, nor does he offer any musical evidence for his interpretation of the character of the seven pavans.

An alternative, complementary rather than contradictory in some respects, draws on the types of melancholy described by Robert Burton in his *Anatomy of Melancholy* (1621) and by other Elizabethan and Jacobean writers.[40] A feature of the English literature on melancholy is its tendency to classify it into a number of distinct types that can be thought of either as phases in the malady that a single individual might suffer or as 'characters' exemplified by different types of individual, as they often were in Jacobean drama. Burton claimed there were no fewer than eighty-eight 'degrees' of melancholy, but the last five of the seven pavans do seem to represent some of the most important types. I believe that these states are reflected to some extent in the character of the pavans.

Melancholy

Melancholy was the fashionable malady of the late Elizabethan age. Burton and his contemporaries diagnosed many causes – social change, political uncertainty, challenges to religious and intellectual certainties, frustrated ambition, or just *fin-de-siècle* malaise – but they agreed that, in the words of John Donne, 'God hath accompanied, and complicated almost all our bodily diseases of these times, with an extraordinary sadnesse, a predominent melancholy, a faintnesse of heart, a chearlesnesse, a joylesnesse of spirit'.[41] They also recognised that melancholy particularly affected Englishmen. Burton diagnosed idleness as a cause, comparing The Netherlands favourably with England, and evoking in the process a series of images startlingly at variance with our modern clichés of the Elizabethan Golden Age:

> those rich United Provinces of Holland, Zealand, &c. over against us; those neat Cities and populous Townes, full of most industrious Artificers, so much land recovered from the Sea, so painefully preserved by those Artificiall inventions . . . so many navigable channels from place to place, made by mens hands, &c. and on the other side so many thousand acres of our Fens lye drowned, our Cities thin, and those vile, poore, and ugly to behold in respect of theirs, our trades decayed, our still running rivers stopped, and that beneficiall use of transportation, wholly

neglected, so many Havens void of Ships and Townes, so many Parkes and Forests for pleasure, barren Heaths, so many villages depopulated, &c. . . . [42]

On the personal level, the Elizabethans used the word 'melancholy' or 'black bile' to describe one of the four liquids or humours thought to be naturally present in the body, as well as the physical and psychological conditions that resulted from an excess of it.[43] The four humours were the bodily equivalents of the four elements of inanimate matter. Black bile was thick, heavy and sluggish, so the melancholy humour was heavy, dull, cold and dry, and was connected with the element earth, the season of winter, old age and, in astrology, the planet Saturn. Thus the melancholy man was lanky, swarthy, taciturn, obstinate, suspicious, jealous and greedy. He naturally preferred solitude and darkness, and was continually tormented by morbid fears and sorrows.

Why the obsession with such an unattractive humour? One reason is simply that melancholy was the fashionable ailment of the age. Dowland certainly cultivated a melancholy public persona. He signed himself 'Jo: dolandi de Lachrimae',[44] gave his pieces titles such as 'Semper Dowland semper Dolens', 'Melancholy Galliard' and 'Forlorn Hope Fancy', and peppered his publications with Latin mottoes such as 'The arts which help all mankind cannot help their master' (the title-page of *The First Booke*) and 'whom Fortune has not blessed, he either rages or weeps' (the title-page of *Lachrimae*).[45] In the emblem book *Parthenia sacra* ([Rouen], 1633; repr. 1971), Henry Hawkins made explicit connections between Dowland, *Lachrimae*, and melancholy when he wrote that a singing bird was more melancholy than 'Dowland himself' in 'al his Plaints and Lachrymies'.[46] Writers, philosophers and scholars were thought to be particularly susceptible to melancholy because they led solitary, sedentary lives, and because concentrated thinking supposedly dried up the body, inducing melancholy. They were also concerned with melancholy because they were able to analyse the malady in all its complexity, and to suggest cures.

Music is important in this respect because it was thought to be one of the most powerful antidotes to melancholy. 'In my judgement', Burton wrote, 'none so present, none so powerfull, none so apposite as a cup of strong drinke, mirth, musicke, and merry company', and went on to explain that music is:

so powerfull a thing, that it ravisheth the soul, *regina sensuum*, the Queene of the sences, by sweet pleasure, (which is an happy cure), and corporall tunes pacifie our incorporeall soule, *sine ore loquens, dominatum in animam exercet* [speaking without a mouth, it exercises domination over the soul], and carries it beyond itselfe, helpes, elevates, extends it.

He also suggested that 'Many men are melancholy by hearing Musicke, but it is a pleasing melancholy that it causeth, and therefore to such as are discontent, in woe, feare, sorrow, or dejected, it is a most present remedy, it expells cares, alters their grieved mindes, and easeth in an instant'.[47] Dowland made a similar point in the *Lachrimae* dedication: 'though the title doth promise teares, unfit guests in these joyfull times, yet no doubt pleasant are the teares which Musicke weepes, neither are teares shed alwayes in sorrowe, but sometime in joy and gladnesse'. One of the functions of his seven pavans, presumably, was to cure the melancholy they so powerfully evoke.

'Lachrimae Antiquae Novae'

If we assume, as I think we can, that 'Antiquae' was written long before Dowland had the idea of expanding its material into a cycle of seven pavans, then it follows that it is an exploration of melancholy in general rather than a single aspect. When it became the first pavan in a cycle of seven it assumed the role of a general introduction to the subject, a point of departure. What then, of 'Antiquae Novae', the 'old-new' tears? I suspect that Dowland also intended this pavan to represent melancholy in general, though the title suggests that the anguish is new or has been renewed in some way.

This is certainly suggested by the music, which is essentially a straightforward revision and elaboration of 'Antiquae'. Some of the ideas, such as the pedal passage at the beginning of the second strain, are simple decorations of the equivalent places in 'Antiquae', but the most striking rhetorical ideas have been moved around, and have been changed in the process. Condensed versions of the figures (c), (d) and (e) are now in the third strain, and have been swapped with the 'Sacred End' motif, which is ingeniously combined in the second strain with a rising figure derived from (a) and, in b. 13 of the Quintus, an inverted version of

Ex. 4.7 'Gementes', bb. 17–20 (lute part omitted)

(b). The harmonic outline of the pavan is essentially the same as 'Anti-quae', though the A cadence at the end of the first strain is extended and therefore reinforced, and the turn into C at the beginning of the second strain is strengthened by replacing the 2–1 motion of the Bassus with a 5–1 motion, and by adding subdominant F major harmony on the first beat of b. 10; it is also prolonged by secondary C cadences in bb. 12–13 and 14–15. This, together with the transfer of the D minor modulation to the third strain (made necessary by moving (c) and (d)), has the effect of greatly lessening the phrygian colour. The result is a more varied, balanced and modern harmonic scheme, an apt illustration of the pavan's title.

'Lachrimae Gementes'

Dowland illustrates 'Gementes', 'sighing, groaning or wailing tears', by a greatly increased use of affective devices. Some of them, such as the startling, declamatory passage near the beginning of the third strain embodying a cadence on E, just serve to raise the temperature in a generalised way. The figure is a classic example of *epizeuxis*, the 'immediate restatement of a word or two for greater vehemency', according to Henry Peacham senior, combined with *mutatio toni*, an abrupt change in harmonic direction for expressive purposes (Ex. 4.7).[48] But others – such as the modified version of the tear motif in bb. 1–2 of the Cantus containing a 5–6–5 motif, the extension of the sequence of falling thirds in bb. 13–14, and the 4–3♯ suspension at the end of the second strain – seem to represent sighing. A number of them – the 5–6–5 sighing motif, the *mutatio toni* and the inconclusive ending to the second strain – are also found in 'I saw my lady weepe', the first song in *The Second Booke*. Daniel Leech-Wilkinson has argued that 'I saw my Lady weepe' was conceived as the first part of a pair with 'Flow my teares', the next piece in the collection.[49] It is in Tone 3 with phrygian leanings, it borrows material from 'Lachrimae', it is also concerned with tears, and it ends inconclusively with a dominant E major cadence that invites resolution by the first chord of 'Flow my teares'.

It is significant that Dowland used the 'Sacred End' figure in all three strains: it is in b. 3 of the Altus, alluded to in bb. 6–7 of the Bassus, developed in imitation in bb. 9–10 of the Cantus and Bassus, and alluded to in bb. 11 and 22–3 of the Altus. Furthermore, the sighing figure that begins the third strain sounds like a modification of the 'Sacred End' figure, and could easily be used to set the same words. I suspect that Dowland spread it throughout the pavan because he was thinking specifically of the sighs and groans of religious melancholy. Burton, a priest himself, considered religious melancholy a species of love melancholy, and went into exhaustive detail, blaming bad diet, fasting, mortification, and solitude as causes.[50] By extension, religious melancholy could include superstition, fanaticism, bigotry, heresy, atheism or hypocrisy.

'Lachrimae Tristes'

Appropriately, 'Tristes', 'Sad Tears', contains the most profoundly sad music. Dowland creates a feeling of grief, despair and even madness in the first two strains mainly by harmonic means, though several dotted crotchet–quaver figures (a grief emblem in later seventeenth-century music) also add to the effect. There are some grinding dissonances in the first strain, such as the minor sevenths between the outer parts on the first beat of b. 3 and the third beat of b. 6 (aggravated by a suspension in the Altus), and the dominant-seventh chord with an added 9–8 suspension on the first beat of b. 7. Furthermore, false relations occur in all but the last two bars of the strain, adding to the hysterical atmosphere. The second strain is more concerned with another type of disorder, harmonic instability. It starts with an unexpected B major chord (a reference to the *mutatio toni* near the beginning of the second strain of 'Gementes'), but

Ex. 4.8 'Tristes', bb. 9–12 (lute part omitted)

rapidly traverses a cycle of fifths to reach G minor two bars later; it outlines the remarkable melodic pattern F♯–G♯–A–B♭–A in bb. 10–11 – a reference to 'I saw my Lady weepe' at the words 'In those faire eies where all perfections keepe' (see Ex. 4.8). There is more disorder at the end of the strain, where the expected phrygian cadence is modified into a strange halting progression involving a bass suspension.

In the third strain, by contrast, the music is almost entirely conventional, though the Altus f′ added to the A minor cadence in b. 20 and the dotted figures in the Cantus at b. 24 are a reminder of what has passed. It is hard to resist the conclusion that Dowland intended this serene music to portray some sort of relief or resolution of grief and despair, particularly since bb. 20–2 are taken up with a rising sequence (another *anabasis* or *ascensio*) using a figure developed from the tear motif that Dowland was to use at the beginning of the much more positive and confident 'Amantis'. As already mentioned, it is similar to the start of Marenzio's 'Rivi, fontane, e fiumi', though it is also a musical commonplace; an obvious example is the passage at the word 'genuite' in the 'Dixit Dominus' of Monteverdi's 1610 *Vespers*.

But what sort of grief and despair is portrayed in 'Tristes'? Writers at the time recognised two main types, sacred and profane, caused respectively by the fear of damnation and rejection in love. Burton wrote that 'The terrible meditation of hell fire and eternall punishment much torments a sinful silly soule', and quoted Martin Luther: 'They doubt of their Election, how they shall know it, by what signes? And so farre forth . . . with such nice points, torture and crucifie themselves, that they are almost mad'. Men possessed with *amor insanus* (mad love), on the other hand, are 'no better than beasts, irrationall, stupid, head-strong, void of feare of God or men, they frequently forsweare themselves, spend, steale, commit incests, rapes, adulteries, murders, depopulate Townes, Citties, Countries, to satisfie their lust'; the mad lover, of course, is a familiar figure in Jacobean drama.[51]

The music of 'Tristes' suggests that it is not primarily concerned with religious despair. If it was, we might expect it to use the 'Sacred End' figure even more than 'Gementes'. It does refer to 'Gementes' in the first strain. The modified 'sighing' version of the tear motif is transferred from the Cantus to the Altus, perhaps to darken the texture, the 'Sacred End' figure is alluded to in bb. 1–2 of the Quintus, and in bb. 5–6 of the Cantus, and two fanfare-like fourths in bb. 5–6 of the Tenor recall the *epizeusis* in bb. 19–20 of 'Gementes'. But much of the melodic material is new, particularly in the second and third strains, and the pavan takes new harmonic directions, hinting at D minor in the first strain and approaching G minor in the second. The beautiful turn into C major in bb. 13–15 is a hint that the pavan is concerned with despairing love, for it is another allusion to 'I saw my Lady weepe', at the words 'to be advanced so'.

'Lachrimae Coactae'

The title, 'enforced tears' or perhaps 'insincere tears' or even 'crocodile tears', suggests a connection with one of the most striking melancholy types: the revenger or malcontent. When the Elizabethan vogue for melancholy began in the 1580s it was associated with Italy, and in particular with Italian travellers or those who affected Italianate manners.[52] Their melancholy was supposedly caused by society's failure to appreciate their talents, or by their dissatisfaction with the *status quo*. Thomas Nashe thought it 'a pitiful thing' that the malcontent

> should take uppe a scornfull melancholy in his gate and countenance, and talke as though our common welth were but a mockery of government, and our Majestrates fooles, who wronged him in not looking into his deserts, not imploying him in State matters, and that, if more regard were not had of him very shortly, the whole Realme should have a misse of him, & he would go (I mary would he) where he should be more accounted of.[53]

Such alienation could easily lead to deceit, intrigue, treachery, sedition, revenge and murder. One wonders whether Dowland was thought to exemplify the melancholy malcontent. He repeatedly complained that his talents went unrecognised in England, he had spent much of his career abroad and had travelled to Italy, and at one stage he was suspected by the authorities of sedition.

Be that as it may, 'Coactae' certainly seems to illustrate the malcontent. It relates mainly to 'Tristes', and can be thought of as a parody of it – in the musical sense as well as the general sense of ironic or satirical exaggeration. It distorts or exaggerates a number of its aspects, just as treachery and revenge pervert grief and despair. For instance, the strange melodic pattern G♯–A–B♭–A in bb. 10–11 of the Cantus of 'Tristes' is reversed, appearing in bb. 6–7 as B♭–A–G♯–A, while the *mutatio toni* at the start of the second strain turns into B minor rather than G minor, the A♯ leading note replacing its enharmonic equivalent, B♭ – a kind of musical irony that would not have been lost on the lutenist, for whom B♭ and A♯ were the same symbol in the tablature.[54] Similarly, the *anabasis* or *ascensio* in bb. 20–2 of 'Tristes' is modified and inverted in bb. 11–13, with an unsettling F♯–F♮ change in the Altus and sinister chromatics in the Bassus. The harmonic instability is maintained almost to the end of the strain: the music swerves to avoid a D minor cadence in b. 14, then apparently heads towards G major but settles into a V–I E major cadence, replacing the expected phrygian cadence. It is perhaps significant that the pavan generally has the most complex part-writing of the set. It starts with the tear motif in close canon between the Cantus and the Quintus, and there is much use of syncopation or *syneresis*, a figure that could be thought of as a musical portrayal of intrigue or deceit, though admittedly no source of the period gives it this interpretation.[55]

'Lachrimae Amantis'

With 'Amantis', 'a lover's tears', the cycle takes a much more positive turn. The tone is set by the Bassus, which marches up a fifth from tonic to dominant, echoing (a) in the process, and then up a seventh, swinging the music into a radiant C major, the first time this key has been reached in the first strain. When the music returns to the home key at the end of the strain, it does so unexpectedly by way of four beats of A major harmony, produced by a sighing A–C♯ sixth in the Bassus and the Altus. Some of the ideas come from 'Tristes', but they are the less anguished ones, or have been modified to seem more joyful and confident. Thus the first three bars are modelled on the *anabasis* or *ascensio* in bb. 20–2 of 'Tristes', while the questing second strain recalls the second strain of 'Tristes', but uses modulations only on the sharp side of the harmonic spectrum; flats are conspicuously avoided, with the exception of the expressive 6♭–3♯ chord in b. 10. Two other features of the pavan contribute to its distinctive character: it conspicuously avoids phrygian progressions, and at the end of each strain the rate of chord-change slows down markedly, producing an oddly static – or even ecstatic – effect. Varying the rate of chord-change was a basic expressive device for the madrigal composer, but it was rarely used in dance music.

We are clearly not dealing here with conventional love melancholy. In the medical tradition deriving from Galen, love melancholy involved sorrow virtually by definition, for erotic love was thought to be a sanguine rather than a melancholy passion; it was warm and moist, produced by an excess of blood in the body. The lover only became cold, dry and melancholic if his love was thwarted. But 'Amantis' is certainly not sorrowful; as Dowland put it, 'neither are tears shed alwayes in sorrowe, but sometime in joy and gladnesse'. The pavan could refer to an alternative tradition, deriving from Aristotle by way of Marsilio Ficino and other humanists, that saw melancholy as noble, virtuous and even inspired. *The Anatomy of Melancholy* is mostly concerned with the Galenic type, but Burton repeated Aristotle's opinion that 'melancholy men of all others are most witty, which causeth many times a divine ravishment, and a kind of *Enthusiasmus*, which stirreth them up to bee excellent Philosophers, Poets, Prophets, &c.'.[56]

Later writers were divided as to how the melancholy humour could produce such contradictory effects, but most agreed, as Robert Crofts put it in 1640, that if melancholics

> Adict themselves to seeke and follow Vertue and Piety (especially if their Melancholly bee with bloud and other good humours moderately humected and allay'd) commonly become of excellent wisdome, sharp Judgements and seeme to doe many things so notably as if they were furthered by some divine Instinct or motion, Insomuch as oft-times even their Solitarinesse and melancholly dispositions become most profitable, sweet and pleasant to them.[57]

Burton presumably had a similar conception of melancholy in mind when he devoted the first few sections of his treatment of love melancholy to its 'natural' and 'rational' aspects, including love of profit, possessions, beauty and 'Charity', which includes 'piety, dilection, benevolence, friendship . . . the love we owe our countrey, nature, wealth, pleasure, honour . . .'.[58] 'Amantis', I suggest, is concerned with these types of virtuous love, not erotic passion.

'Lachrimae Verae'

'Verae', 'true tears', seems to be concerned with a more specific aspect of noble melancholy, the 'divinest Melancholy' of the scholar and philosopher, later celebrated by John Milton. In his poem 'L'Allegro' he rejects the Galenic type, 'loathed Melancholy / Of Cerberus, and blackest midnight born', in favour of 'heart-easing Mirth'. But Babb argued that the companion poem, 'Il Penseroso', is an extended exploration of Aristotelian melancholy. Milton personifies it as a 'Goddes, sage and holy', a 'pensive Nun, devout and pure, / Sober, stedfast and demure'. Under her influence the poet is a wide-ranging seeker after truth and beauty, contemplating nature, studying philosophy, appreciating tragic drama, poetry, religious architecture and church music, before studying astronomy and botany in retirement in his 'Mossy Cell' until 'old experience do attain / To something like Prophetic strain'.[59]

There certainly seems to be a wide-ranging quality to 'Verae', in part because it tends to summarise and recapitulate the preceding pavans, and is therefore more varied than any one of them. It begins with a variant of the contrapuntal treatment of the tear motif, deriving from bb. 20–2 of 'Tristes' by way of the opening of 'Amantis'. In b. 4 it swerves unexpectedly into G minor, recalling b. 11 of 'Tristes', and the B♭–A–G♯–A figure in the Cantus at the end of the strain is a direct reference to 'Coactae', bb. 6–7. The second strain refers again to the contrapuntal treatment of the tear motif, with the bass marching upwards in crotchets as in the opening of 'Amantis', and the D major–B major transition in 'Amantis', b. 12, is echoed by the unexpected change in b. 10 from a G major cadence to E major harmony, while the progression in bb. 11–12 cunningly combines the 6♭–3♯ chord in 'Amantis', b. 10, with the G♯–A–B♭–A figure in 'Tristes', bb. 10–11.[60] The end of the strain returns to a phrygian cadence

Ex. 4.9 'Verae', bb. 17–24 (lute part omitted)

on E, referring back to the first three pavans, though the 4–3♯ suspension relates it particularly to 'Gementes'. 'Amantis' is the main source of the third strain: its A–C♯ sixths in bb. 6–7 have their counterparts in the E–G♯ sixths in the Tenor, Bassus and Cantus parts of bb. 17–18, while its opening is referred to yet again in bb. 19–20. Furthermore, the static effect I observed towards the end of each strain of 'Amantis' is taken a stage further in the last four bars of 'Verae'. There is only one chord to a bar, and several internal cadences are avoided, producing a strange visionary, trance-like effect – a prophetic strain indeed (see Ex. 4.9).

Much more could be said about the seven pavans, though we can now see that they form a true cycle, cumulative in its effect and greater than the sum of its parts. They demand to be performed in a sequence, though each pavan makes perfect sense on its own. They are linked by a subtle web of melodic and harmonic cross-references, but they also seem to outline a coherent spiritual programme taking the listener from conventional, non-specific sadness through religious melancholy, grief and despair, alienation and revenge, heroic and virtuous love, to enlightenment and wisdom.

5

'Divers other Pavans, Galiards, and Almands'

The ordering of the collection

We have seen that the first part of *Lachrimae*, the seven 'Passionate Pavans', has a complex and subtle organisation. But what of the second part? At first sight it seems to be a miscellaneous collection. Dowland described the fourteen other dances just as 'divers other Pavans, Galiards, and Almands' on the title-page, and described *Lachrimae* in the preface as 'this long and troublesome worke, wherein I have mixed new songs with olde, grave with light'. Nevertheless, method can be detected in the ordering of *Lachrimae* on several levels.

The most obvious is that the collection contains twenty-one dances: ten pavans, nine galliards and two almands. Many vocal collections of the period have this number of pieces, including Dowland's *Third and Last Booke* and *A Pilgrimes Solace*, Bartlet's *Booke of Ayres* (1606), Campion's *Two Bookes of Ayres* (?1613), Greaves's *Songs of Sundrie Kindes* (1604), all five of Robert Jones's song books (1600, 1601, 1608, 1609, 1610), and the double *Booke of Ayres* published by Campion and Rosseter (1601), as well as Carleton's *Madrigals* (1601), Farnaby's *Canzonets to Fowre Voyces* (1598), and three collections by Morley, *The First Booke of Canzonets to Two Voyces* (1595), *The First Booke of Balletts* (1595) and *Canzonets or Little Short Aers* (1597). It is also common in Italian madrigal collections. To take just those by Dowland's idol Marenzio, his four-part book, his third, fourth, seventh, eighth, and ninth five-part books, and his second, third, fifth, and sixth six-part books all have twenty-one pieces, as does his first book of *madrigali spirituali*.[1]

Why is this so? An obvious possibility is that the number twenty-one has a symbolic significance, since it combines the numerologically significant numbers seven and three, and the number seven is expressed both in the cycle of seven pavans and, if we accept Lionel Pike's argument (see Chapter 4), the harmonies of 'Lachrimae' itself. But twenty-one does not seem to be a particularly significant number itself, and a more likely explanation is that it is a convenient number for printed collections.[2] A quarto part-book of a madrigal set will typically consist of twenty-four pages made up of three gatherings of eight pages, so twenty-one pieces taking a page each will leave space for preliminaries such as a title-page, a dedication, and a preface. Similar calculations apply to *Lachrimae* and other table layout books in folio. Twenty-one pieces each taking up an opening account for forty-two pages, leaving six pages for preliminaries. Dowland used only five pages for preliminaries in *Lachrimae* – title-page, Latin dedication, English dedication, preface 'To the Reader', and table of contents – though the book actually runs to forty-nine pages because 'Dolens' is too long for a single opening. Luckily, it was possible to tip in an odd leaf at the beginning or the end, which probably explains why some collections consist of twenty-two pieces. Examples include Dowland's *First Booke*, East's *Second Set of Madrigales* (1606) and his *Third Set of Bookes* (1610), and Pilkington's *First Booke of Songs or Ayres* (1605).

Lachrimae is initially ordered by genre, progressing from the slowest and most serious pieces, the pavans, to the fastest and lightest, the almands. The principle can be detected in many sixteenth-century collections, though an element of grouping by key was also increasingly common. In Holborne's *Pavans, Galliards, Almains*, for instance, pavan and galliard pairs are followed by almands and corants. By the early seventeenth century collections were usually organised by key rather than genre: apart from two separate pieces, Schein's *Banchetto musicale* (Leipzig, 1617) consists of twenty five-movement suites.[3]

Thus *Lachrimae* is highly unusual among contemporary consort collections in that the principle of grouping by genre takes precedence over the desire to pair pieces by key. Indeed, Dowland seems to have gone out of his way to avoid pairing pavans and galliards. He did not provide any galliards in the same keys as 'Dolens' or 'Langton', and while 'Unton' is in Tone 2 and therefore could be paired with the Tone 2 'Essex', 'Noel', 'Collier' or 'Piper', there is no reason to connect it with any of them. 'Collier' could not be easily paired with 'Unton', since, as we saw in Chapter 2, it is scored differently, with two equal soprano parts, while the proper pair for 'Piper', the related five-part 'Piper's Pavan', was left out of the collection; it is in D-Kl, 4° MS mus. 125, 1–5.[4] Presumably Dowland preferred the more interesting and original relationships he had developed between 'Antiquae' and the other 'Lachrimae' pavans. Nevertheless, Dowland does seem to have chosen or composed some of his 'divers other Pavans, Galiards, and Almands' so that they relate in some way to the seven 'Lachrimae' pavans.

A second principle can be detected in the 'divers other Pavans, Galiards, and Almands'. It can be seen most clearly in the sequence of galliards: they are ordered according to the rank of the dedicatee.[5] Thus a piece dedicated to a king, 'Denmark', is followed by ones named after an earl, 'Essex', a knight, 'Souch', and then six commoners. Similarly, a pavan dedicated to a knight, 'Unton', takes precedence over 'Langton', dedicated to a commoner, though the position of 'Dolens' at the head of the three 'divers other Pavans' could be read as an assertion of the dignity of the artist over worldly rank, if we accept that the pavan is, in a sense, dedicated to himself.

Be that as it may, *Lachrimae* is unusual in that the 'Divers other Pavans, Galiards, and Almands' are all dedicated to different people, and it is striking how many of them are relatively unknown. Taken with the fact that in at least three cases the pieces seem to be memorials to the recently deceased, it looks as if the dedications are records of personal friendship or esteem, along the lines of the 'friends pictured within' Elgar's *Enigma Variations*, rather than attempts to curry favour among the great and the good. This in turn raises the possibility that, like Elgar, Dowland matched the mood of each piece to the character of its dedicatee, or matched the dedicatee to the mood of the piece, for it seems that some of them were only named when they appeared in *Lachrimae*. Perhaps future research will reveal more about the more obscure figures he chose, and thus more about the music Dowland dedicated to them.

'Semper Dowland semper Dolens'

'Dolens' comes after 'Verae', and to some extent acts as a pendant to the 'Lachrimae' pavans, which is why, Warwick Edwards suggested, Dowland chose to work in several allusions to his song 'Go christall teares' from *The First Booke*.[6] Diana Poulton suggested that Dowland

Ex. 5.1 'Dolens', bb. 7–9 (lute part omitted)

derived its title, literally 'always Dowland, always sorrowful', from the Latin motto 'Doleo, quia semper dolens dolere nescio' ('I sorrow because, ever sorrowing, I know not how to sorrow'), copied in December 1602 by the barrister John Manningham from a French work on civil law, but David Pinto has suggested to me that it ultimately derives from a phrase of St Augustine, 'dolerem, quia non legerem quod dolerem' ('how sorry would I be, for that I might not read that which would make me sorry').[7]

'Dolens' seems to portray Dowland's personal anguish in a way that the 'Lachrimae' pavans do not, concerned as they are with the various 'characters' of melancholy; indeed, the piece seems to be much more of a self-portrait than 'Antiquae' or 'Antiquae Novae', an exploration of Dowland's own melancholy character. Significantly, the connections are mostly with 'Tristes'. Both pavans open with sighing suspended figures that refer to 'Go christall teares', and the *modulatio toni* outlining the G♯–A–B♭ figure in the Cantus of bb. 10–11 of 'Tristes' is echoed by bb. 7–8 of 'Dolens' (see Ex. 5.1). Also, the dotted-crotchet–quaver figures I remarked on in the former are developed into a full-blown contrapuntal figure at the end of the second strain of the latter.

However, the most striking feature of 'Dolens' is its harmonic instability. Dowland seems to have set out to make it as difficult as possible to determine its tonality. It continually twists and turns between Tones 1, 2 and 3, false relations constantly cancel the effect of the leading notes of internal cadences, and each strain breaks off with an unexpected inconclusive cadence, leaving the music in the air – a device perhaps inspired by the similar cadence at the end of the second strain of 'Gementes'. It is the musical equivalent of *aposiopesis*, the rhetorical device that Henry Peacham senior described as 'when through some affection, as of feare, anger, sorrow, bashfulnesse, and such like, we break of[f] our speech, before it all be ended'.[8]

The reader will be aware by now that I believe 'Dolens' was written especially for *Lachrimae*, and that the lute solo, with its disappointingly conventional final cadence, is not the original as Diana Poulton suggested; perhaps it was altered by someone who could not stomach Dowland's inconclusive ending.[9] I find it hard to believe that this striking effect, used so memorably at the end of the song 'In darknesse let me dwell' in *A Musicall Banquet*, was not part of his original conception, though two sources of the lute setting, The Euing Lute Book and The Weld Lute Book, are usually dated around 1600, and therefore appear to predate *Lachrimae*. But this is just a guess: the Euing book was probably copied nearer 1610 than 1600, and the Weld book could easily date from a year or two after 1603–4.[10] With strains of ten, eleven and fifteen bars, 'Dolens' is by far Dowland's longest pavan, and its third strain, with a synthetic cantus firmus in the manner of Philips's 1580 Pavan (see Chapter 3), contains some of his most complex and sophisticated counterpoint.

'Sir Henry Umptons Funerall'

The two remaining pavans in *Lachrimae* are shorter and simpler works, and seem to be earlier. 'Unton' is unique to the collection: there is no separate lute setting, perhaps because the *Lachrimae* lute part has all the essential melodic material and works well as a solo; perhaps it was conceived as such. The piece is a memorial to the diplomat Sir Henry Unton or Umpton of Wadley near Faringdon in Berkshire (*d.* 23 March 1596), and is therefore the counterpart to a collection of Latin verse, *Funebria nobilissimi ad praestantissimi equitis D. Henrici Untoni* (Oxford, 1596), and the famous biographical painting, now in the National Portrait Gallery, that includes depictions of a mixed consort and a five-part viol consort.[11]

Warwick Edwards first pointed out that 'Unton' has virtually the same harmonic plan as a pavan by Holborne, 'The Funerals' in *Pavans, Galliards, Almains*, no. 31, entitled more precisely 'The Countess of Pembroke's Funeral' in the lute setting – presumably Anne, second wife of William Herbert, first Earl of Pembroke (*d.* 8 August 1588).[12] Thus

Dowland seems to have borrowed from Holborne rather than the other way round, and this is borne out by the music. Holborne's pavan is relatively simple, with three eight-bar strains and rather loosely organised counterpoint mainly in plain patterns of rising and falling crotchets, while Dowland's is much more elaborate, with the third strain extended to ten bars, and several sections of complex imitative counterpoint. Two of them are related to ideas in 'Antiquae': bb. 6–7 is another version of the 'Sacred End' figure, with its appropriate associations with the words 'Mercie, good Lord, mercie', while bb. 13–14 uses the contrapuntal version of the tear motif derived from the opening of Marenzio's 'Rivi, fontane, e fiumi'. I believe that Dowland intended this idea to represent consolation and relief from sorrow in 'Tristes', and it presumably has the same meaning here.

'M. John Langtons Pavan'

It has often been suggested that pavans named after individuals were written as memorial pieces, and while 'Unton' seems to confirm the theory, 'Langton' contradicts it: the Lincolnshire landowner John Langton (1561–1616) of Langton near Horncastle was very much alive in 1604, and the piece is Dowland's least sorrowful pavan, in a sunny Tone 6.[13] Zarlino wrote that its ancestor, the lydian fifth mode, 'brings to the spirit modesty, happiness, and relief from annoying cares', and that the moderns, 'induced by the sweetness and beauty' of the ionian eleventh mode, replace b-natural with b-flat – effectively creating F major.[14] The pavan exists in three versions, an early untitled lute pavan, the *Lachrimae* consort setting, and a later lute setting in *Varietie of Lute-Lessons* entitled 'Sir John Langton his Pavin' – Langton was knighted in 1603.[15] The first two are fairly similar, but 'Sir John Langton his Pavin' has more elaborate divisions, and in it Dowland took the opportunity to correct the strange rhythmic displacement in the second half of the second strain which shifts the internal cadences on to the second and fourth beats of the bar. He inserted an extra minim into b. 10 and three minims into b. 13, creating an eight-bar rather than a seven-bar strain, thus avoiding the awkward effect in b. 14, where the dominant harmony arrives a beat early and has to be artificially prolonged.

This suggests that 'Langton' is a fairly early work, and it is borne out by the simple, Holborne-like style and the limited harmonic plan, I–I / V–V / I–I. Paul O'Dette has remarked on Dowland's fondness for beginning pieces with melodies that descend a fifth by step,[16] though Holborne also used the idea several times: Pavan no. 3 of *Pavans, Galliards, Almains* begins in virtually the same way as 'Langton'. Nevertheless, 'Langton' is a sweetly satisfying work, with a number of felicitous touches, such as the tiny rising imitative point in bb. 3–4, the unexpected C minor chord on the fourth beat of b. 4 (not present in the lute settings), and the opening of the third strain, which contains a beautiful harmonic turn similar to bb. 13–14 of 'Awake sweete love' in *The First Booke*.[17] For some reason the first bar of the second strain is virtually the same as the equivalent bar in the lute pavan 'La mia Barbara'.[18]

'The Earle of Essex Galiard'

Dowland was evidently particularly fond of the galliard as a genre. We know of more than thirty examples by him, and there are nine in *Lachrimae*. Among them are some of his most popular pieces: all but two are known in earlier instrumental versions, and four also exist as songs. It is not clear whether 'Essex' was written before its song version, 'Can she excuse my wrongs' in *The First Booke*. The earliest datable source, the Dowland Lutebook in Washington (*c.* 1594), includes a lute setting signed by the composer with the title 'Can she excuse', which implies that the song version was circulating by then.[19] But Edward Doughtie pointed out that the poem, supposedly Essex's complaint against Queen Elizabeth, has no proper metrical structure, and produces unnatural word stresses when sung, a sure sign that the dance came first.[20] Furthermore, the vigorous and forth-right music, a study in galliard cross-rhythms, is rather at odds with the mood of the text, though it is an apt portrait of the dashing and impulsive earl. So far as we know, Dowland first used the title 'The Earle of Essex Galiard' in *Lachrimae*, perhaps to commemorate Essex's execution in 1601. But he may have had him in mind from the beginning, for the Altus quotes the popular song 'Will you go walk the woods so wild' in the third strain, which may be a subtle reference to

Essex's fondness for his country house at Wanstead in Epping Forest; John Ward pointed out that the tune was often quoted in contrapuntal compositions.[21]

'Captaine Digorie Piper his Galiard'

'Piper' is strikingly similar to 'Essex', and was occasionally confused with it at the time. They are both in Tone 2 with phrygian leanings, they both consist of three eight-bar strains, and they start with arching phrases that rise in arpeggios and then fall by step to a dominant chord on the first beat of b. 4. Yet if 'Piper' is a portrait of the notorious Captain Digorie Piper (1559–90) of *The Sweepstake* who narrowly escaped punishment for piracy in 1586, he was a more sombre character than the Earl of Essex.[22] The piece demands a slower tempo, there is a noticeable absence of jaunty cross-rhythms, and the potentially lively figure in the third strain is made more subdued by the absence of the bass in the first four bars. Of course, this may just be because the song version, 'If my complaints could passions move', was written first. The text makes good sense as a poem and fits the tune well, though there are signs that at least the lower vocal parts of the part-song version were added later: their underlay is often awkward, and Dowland had to fudge the imitative entry in b. 2 of the tenor part. The evidence of the sources is not conclusive: Dowland may have composed the solo lute version by the time Piper died in 1590, since Matthew Holmes copied it into GB–Cu, MS Dd.2.11, f. 53 in the early 1590s, while the song is in *The First Booke* of 1597.[23]

'M. Henry Noel his Galiard'

Like 'Essex' and 'Piper', 'Noel' also exists as a lute solo and a song as well as the *Lachrimae* consort setting. The lute solo, entitled 'Mignarde' or 'Mignarda', is in GB–Cu, MS Dd.2.11, f. 77,[24] which means it was in circulation in the early 1590s, while the song, 'Shall I strive with wordes to move', only appeared in *A Pilgrimes Solace* of 1612. This suggests it was originally written as an instrumental galliard rather than a song, and this is borne out by the fact that, like 'Flow my teares', 'Shall I strive with wordes to move' has no metrical regularity, and some of the accentuation of the words is, for Dowland, surprisingly clumsy.[25] The title 'Mignarde', a French-derived word meaning 'delicate', 'pretty' or 'mincing', is apt for a graceful piece similar in mood to 'Piper'; Arbeau used the word 'mignardez', 'delicately', 'prettily' or 'mincingly' to describe an especially graceful way of executing the five steps of the galliard.[26] Dowland probably changed its title in *Lachrimae* to commemorate his friend and patron, the courtier Henry Noel, who died in February 1597.[27]

'Sir John Souch his Galiard'

'Souch', by contrast, probably started life as the song 'My thoughts are wingd with hopes' in *The First Booke*. The poem is in regular iambic pentameters, and was clearly not written to fit the music, since it circulated independently of the song and has been attributed to John Lyly, George earl of Cumberland and Walter Ralegh, among others. Diana Poulton pointed out that the melody seems to be a response to the first verse – the words 'mount', 'moone' and 'the heavens' are set to high notes – and Anthony Munday wrote verses published in 1584 to fit the vocal form of the melody.[28] The earliest source of the instrumental version of the melody, which is more decorated than the song in the second and third strains, seems to be an untitled lute solo in GB-Cu, Dd. 5.78.3, dating from the 1590s; the dedication to Sir John Souch or Zouch of Codnor Castle in Derbyshire is only found in *Lachrimae*.[29]

The galliard is of interest for its connections with 'Antiquae'. It is in Tone 3, it has essentially the same harmonic pattern as the pavan, with phrygian cadences in bb. 3–4, 15–16 and 19–20 and a prominent turn into C major at the beginning of the second strain, and the melody includes the tetrachord C–B–A–G♯ a number of times. John Ward has also pointed out that it belongs to a family of English galliards that begin in a similar way, including Daniel Bacheler's song 'To plead my faith', Dowland's 'Queen Elizabeth's Galliard', and a popular galliard by the court wind player James Harding, as well as 'Hoby' in *Lachrimae*.[30]

'M. Giles Hobies his Galiard'

In fact, 'Hoby' is virtually a parody of James Harding's galliard: the two pieces have similar harmonic patterns, and there are a number

Ex. 5.2a J. Harding, Galliard, bb. 12–16

Ex. 5.2b 'Hoby', bb. 20–4 (lute part omitted)

of significant melodic details in common, such as the passage of cross-rhythms at the beginning of the second strain, and the syncopated rising pattern at the end of Harding's second strain, which Dowland placed at the end of his third strain (see Ex. 5.2). Perhaps Dowland was just returning the compliment, for James Harding may have written his galliard to be paired with 'Lachrimae'. The two pieces are found together a number of times, including Byrd's keyboard setting and the five-part one copied by William Wigthorpe, while 'Can she excuse' / 'Essex' was also sometimes pressed into service in the same way; 'Lachrimae' did not have its own galliard until the lute 'Galliard to Lachrimae' appeared in *A Pilgrimes Solace* in 1612.[31] Dowland probably gave 'Hoby' its title only when he published it in *Lachrimae* (an earlier lute setting is untitled), though little is known about Giles Hoby (1565–1626) of the Herefordshire landed family, and nothing about why Dowland dedicated this splendidly vigorous piece to him.[32]

'M. Buctons Galiard'

'Bucton' is also a reworking of music by another composer. It is one of four galliards associated with Dowland that are derived from Lassus's famous chanson 'Susane un jour', first published in London in 1570.[33] The others are the early anonymous lute piece 'Suzanna Galliard', the five-part 'Galliard / Jhon Douland' in the 1607 Füllsack and Hilde-brandt anthology, and the later lute piece dedicated to Sir Robert Sidney, 'The Right Honourable the Lord Viscount Lisle, His Galliard' in *Varietie of Lute-Lessons*. The four pieces were boiled down surprisingly literally from the original; indeed, virtually every note of 'Bucton' derives from Lassus. The first strain comes from bb. 1–6 and 13–14, the second strain from bb. 28–9, 31–4 and 46–9, while the third strain comes from the chanson's final phrase, b. 53 to the end. This technique of deriving dances from French chansons went back to the early sixteenth century, and was outmoded by 1604; two equivalent pieces, five-part pavans based rather more loosely on 'Susane un jour' by Alfonso Ferrabosco I and Joseph Lupo, may have been written as early as the 1570s.[34]

'Bucton' is the closest of the four galliards to the chanson, since Lassus's tune tends to be obscured by decorations in the lute settings, and the Cantus of the other five-part setting is also decorated with lute-like figuration, perhaps derived from an otherwise lost lute piece. It is also much more subtle than the others, and may therefore be the latest, though it was published earlier than two of them. For instance, their openings are homophonic, while it begins with elaborate counterpoint, and the beginning of its third strain is greatly enhanced by allowing the tune to get out of step with the lower parts, creating a delightful type of rhythmic counterpoint (see Ex. 5.3). John Ward suggested that the dedicatee of this small masterpiece was a courier who worked with Dowland for Sir Henry Cobham in Paris.[35]

'The King of Denmarks Galiard'

'Denmark' is also a compilation, drawn from the repertory of Renaissance battle music. It consists of three four-bar phrases with written-out varied repeats, of which the first two (A, B) are closely related, embodying Dowland's favourite melodic descent from fifth to tonic, while the

Ex. 5.3 'Bucton', bb. 17–21 (lute part omitted)

third (C) begins with an ascending dotted phrase. All three relate to passages in two English keyboard battle pieces, the 'March of Horsemen' section of William Byrd's 'The Battle' and 'A Battle and no Battle' attributed to John Bull, while A and B also relate to passages in an anonymous lute battle piece, found in the Dallis lute manuscript of 1583 and several later sources.[36] Dowland also used A and C as the second and third strains of 'Mr. Langton's Galliard', while another galliard attributed to him begins with A in the minor rather than the major; Dowland's 'Round Battle Galliard' is not related.[37]

In essence, the three phrases are decorations of the same harmony, I–V–I or I–IV–V–I, and they appear in 'A Battle and no Battle' as part of a set of divisions on a ground, with the ground allocated to a second player. But 'Denmark' is different from the other pieces in that each phrase is in a different key – D major, F major and D minor – and this striking device evidently impressed Charles Butler, who mentioned 'the Battel-galliard' as an example of how different modes could be 'compounded' or mixed together in a single piece.[38] The late lute setting in *Varietie of Lute-Lessons* preserves the three-key structure of 'Denmark' but adds three beautifully conceived and imaginative variations.[39] Dowland presumably intended his battle piece as a compliment to Christian IV's military prowess, though the king was to be notably unsuccessful as a commander in the Thirty Years War. Its warlike character could also be a sly reference to Christian's reputation as a hard drinker, for the Danish king's toasts were habitually accompanied by trumpets and drums, as in the first act of *Hamlet*: 'And as he dreines his draughts of Rhenish downe, / The kettle Drum and Trumpet thus bray out / The triumph of his Pledge'.[40] Perhaps Dowland also intended the key changes to represent drunkenness.

'M. Thomas Collier his Galiard with 2 Trebles'

The two galliards still to be discussed, 'Gryffith' and 'Collier', do not survive in any other source, and may have been written specially for *Lachrimae*. 'Collier' is much the simpler of the two, with three eight-bar strains, and could easily have been taken for an early piece had Dowland not used the new-fangled two-soprano scoring. Yet the musical potential of this device is only really exploited in the third strain, when the soprano instruments engage in a proper dialogue using material similar to, and perhaps derived from, the third strain of 'Piper'. Nothing is known of Thomas Collier.

'M. Nicholas Gryffith his Galiard'

'Gryffith' is virtually the only galliard in the repertory with the sort of elaborate imitative counterpoint we associate with pavans. Dowland gave himself the space to achieve this partly by extending the second and third strains to twelve bars, and partly by speeding up the harmonic rhythm, which inevitably slows down the tempo. It is largely taken up with patterns of rising and falling crotchets, sometimes incorporating the contrapuntal version of the tear motif used in 'Tristes', 'Amantis' and 'Verae'. Though it shares Tone 3 with the seven 'Lachrimae' pavans, it is interesting and perhaps significant that its tonality is as different from them as it is possible to be. While they lean towards the phrygian Tone 4, it shows the strong influence of Tone 1: it starts with an A major rather than an A minor chord, there are internal D minor cadences in the first and third strains, and the second strain is largely in D minor, eventually cadencing in the distant key of F major – one of the 'Improper Cadences', 'strange and informal to the Air' and 'sparingly to be used', according to Charles Butler. It is hard to believe that Dowland wrote his most complex and sophisticated galliard much before *Lachrimae* was published, though we can only guess why he dedicated it to the obscure Nicholas Gryffith or Griffith, M.P. for Carnarvon.[41]

'Mistresse Nichols Almand'

Lachrimae ends with the two almands, 'Nichol' and 'Whitehead'. They are both in Tone 5, but are quite different from each other. The former is a breezy little two-strain piece of just twelve four-crotchet bars. The *Lachrimae* version, the only one dedicated to the otherwise unknown Mistress Nichol or Nichols, is more complex than the simple lute setting, with a series of suspensions in the last four bars. It may have existed before 1604, or there may have been an intermediate version, now lost, for the five-part setting in Valentin Haussmann's *Rest von Polnischen und andern Täntzen* (Nuremberg, 1603), published before *Lachrimae* appeared, has some of its features, including the suspensions in the last four bars.[42]

'M. George Whitehead his Almand'

'Whitehead' is much more extended and sophisticated, with strains of eight and sixteen bars, a wide-ranging tonal scheme with modulations to G major, D minor, A minor and F major, and a remarkable question-and-answer passage in the second strain that sounds like battle music. Diana Poulton suggests it was influenced by a four-part chant of the Athanasian Creed in an Oxford manuscript, but chants of this sort only developed after the Restoration, and the manuscript dates from around 1700.[43] 'Whitehead' is not known elsewhere, and was probably written specially for the volume; again, we do not know why Dowland dedicated it to George Whitehead, an obscure tenant of the Duke of Northumberland.[44]

6

Reception

John Dowland was a prophet largely without honour in his own land. He was one of the most famous lutenists in Europe, yet he had to wait until he was nearly fifty before he received a post at the English court. He was one of the greatest English composers of his time, yet his music was quickly forgotten by his compatriots. The lute song was superseded in the 1620s by new types of continuo song. The brilliant and elaborate type of lute music he cultivated gave way about the same time to slighter and less demanding idioms from France using the new Baroque tunings. And the great idiom of Elizabethan consort dance music, brought to its highest point by Dowland, was quickly replaced by new forms and styles. The pavan and the galliard gave way to new and lighter dances such the almand, corant and saraband, scored for lighter and smaller combinations of violins and viols with theorboes. Although some Jacobean consort music continued to be copied until after the Restoration, none of the *Lachrimae* pieces exists in later English sources.

However, Dowland's music survived for rather longer in the Anglo-German consort repertory. Thomas Simpson included settings of 'Antiquae Novae' and 'Langton' in his *Opusculum neuwer Pavanen*, pairing them with his own related galliards; Konrad Hagius printed his own setting of 'Essex' in his partly lost *Newe künstliche musicalische Intraden* (Nuremberg, 1616), wrongly entitling it 'Pypers Galliard'; and Simpson included a version of 'Nichol' in *Taffel-Consort* (Hamburg, 1621), using the new 'string quartet' scoring of two sopranos, tenor and bass with a continuo part rather than Dowland's five-part scoring with a single soprano.[1] Other Dowland pieces in German consort collections include the pavan 'La mia Barbara' in Simpson's *Opusculum*, two settings of 'Piper' printed by Hagius, and arrangements in *Taffel-Consort* of the songs 'Were every thought an eye' and 'Lady if you so spite me', as well as a pavan and a volta ascribed to Dowland but not known else-where.[2]

The Anglo–German consort style petered out in the 1620s, prob-ably because the Thirty Years War had begun to limit the access of English touring theatre companies to Germany, but a few pieces by Dowland survived longer in the keyboard repertory. We have English settings of 'Lachrimae' by William Byrd, Giles Farnaby, William Randall and Benjamin Cosyn, among others, and the piece probably entered the German repertory partly by way of Sweelinck's 'Pavana Lachrymae': his pupil Melchior Schildt wrote a setting, and an anony-mous one has been attributed to Heinrich Scheidemann, another pupil.[3] A fragment of the Schildt setting is in a Swedish manuscript started in 1641 that also includes a setting of 'La mia Barbara' pavan by Paul Siefert, a third Sweelinck pupil, while the only source of the Sweelinck 'Pavana Lachrymae', now in Budapest, may date from 1670 or later; it also includes keyboard variations on 'Denmark' by Samuel Scheidt, yet another Sweelinck pupil.[4] Scheidt's famous five-part 'Galliard Battaglia', printed in 1621, also takes 'Denmark' as its start-ing point.[5]

Dowland's memory was also preserved for several decades after his death by pieces that allude in various ways to 'Lachrimae'. The prac-tice of writing pavans beginning with the tear motif began quite early. Holborne used it to begin six pavans in *Pavans, Galliards, Almains*, nos. 7, 21 'Infernum', 23 'Spero', 27 'The Image of Melancholy', 49 'Plo-ravit' and 51 'Posthuma', and it is also found in five-part pavans by Thomas Weelkes and George Kirbye, an incomplete five-part pavan by Tomkins, a five-part pavan and galliard by Brade in Füllsack and Hildebrandt's 1607 anthology, a six-part pavan in Brade's 1614 collec-tion, a five-part pavan and galliard in Simpson's 1610 collection, the pavan from the Suite no. 6 in Schein's *Banchetto musicale*, and the pavan for four crumhorns in the same collection.[6] Pieces of this sort for solo instruments include the Landgrave of Hesse's eloquent lute pavan dedicated to Dowland and printed in *Varietie of Lute-Lessons*, a key-board pavan and galliard by Morley beginning with the complete tear motif, and Orlando Gibbons's 'Lord Salisbury' pavan and galliard; another keyboard pavan by Orlando Gibbons does not use the falling fourth, but alludes to the harmony of 'Lachrimae' in several places, and uses the idea that begins Dowland's third strain at the beginning of the second strain.[7]

Many later pieces also use the tear motif, though it is hard to know whether their composers were responding directly to 'Lachrimae' or just generally to a tradition of sorrowful pavans derived from it. They include a four-part pavan in D minor by William Lawes, rewritten by him in C minor for five viols and organ; the opening of Lawes's Fantasia Suite no. 7 in D minor for two violins, bass viol and organ; a four-part pavan in D minor by John Jenkins; and a four-part D-minor pavan by the Hamburg violinist Johann Schop (c. 1590–1667), probably a pupil of William Brade.[8] The last alludes to 'Lachrimae' at the beginning of the first two strains, and then quotes the opening of 'Langton' at the beginning of the third. Schop's music preserved elements of the Anglo-German style long after most of his contemporaries had moved on to other things: his divisions on 'Lachrimae' for violin and bass was published in 't Uitnement Kabinet I (Amsterdam, 1646).[9] The falling tetrachords of 'Lachrimae' are also echoed in a group of late seventeenth-century French lute allemandes or allemande-like tombeaux by Jacques Gallot, Robert de Visée and Charles Mouton, as well as Germans working in the same tradition such as Esias Reusner and Silvius Leopold Weiss.[10]

Dowland's music lingered longest in The Netherlands: the tunes of four of his pieces – 'Lachrimae', 'Now, O now I needs must part' or the 'Frog Galliard', the country dance version of 'Essex' or 'Can she excuse' (see below), and 'Come againe, sweet love doth now envite' – passed into the Dutch repertory of popular songs, probably from travelling English theatre troupes. All four appear in Adriaen Valerius's Neder-landtsche gedenck-clanck (Haarlem, 1626; repr. 1974), and the first three were printed in successive editions of Stichtelycke rymen by Dirk Rafaelszoon Camphuysen.[11] Valerius printed a setting of 'Lachrimae' for two voices with lute and cittern, while it appeared in the 1647 edition of Stichtelycke rymen set for four voices, and in the 1652 edition set for two voices with variations by Joseph Butler for violin and bass viol. Its popularity also ensured it a place in instrumental anthologies such as Nicolas Vallet's Apollinis süsse Leyr (Amsterdam, 1642) and Jacob van Eyck's Euterpe (Amsterdam, 1644), reprinted in Der fluyten lust-hof I (Amsterdam, 1649); the former is a setting for violin and bass (the violin part is lost), the latter four variations for solo recorder. The tune is found in Dutch song books up to 1743.

'Essex' or 'Can she excuse' also survived into the eighteenth century, but in a country dance version known as 'Excuse me', first printed in Thomas Robinson's *New Citharen Lessons* (1609), no. 21. Van Eyck published two settings as 'Excusemoy' in *Der Fluyten Lust-hof* II (Amsterdam, 1646), and it appeared in Dutch sources as late as *Oude en nieuwe Hollantse boren lietjes en contredansen* (Amsterdam, *c.* 1700–*c.* 1716; repr. 1972). 'Excuse me' is the only tune deriving from Dowland that also survived in the English popular repertory: it appeared in *The Dancing Master* from the seventh edition (1686) to the eighteenth (*c.* 1728), and was also called for in several ballad operas, including Gay's *Polly* (1729) and Andrew Barton's *The Disappointment, or The Force of Credulity* (New York, 1767).[12]

Revival

The 1760s saw the beginnings of the revival of Elizabethan music. The first volume of Boyce's *Cathedral Music* appeared in 1760, and Sir John Hawkins and Charles Burney were actively collecting material during the decade for their rival histories of music, published respectively in 1776 and 1776, 1782 and 1789. Hawkins confined himself to an outline of Dowland's life, and although Burney attempted to assess the music, he was notably unsympathetic: he claimed to have been 'equally disappointed and astonished' at Dowland's 'scanty abilities in counterpoint, and the great reputation he acquired with his co[n]temporaries', and suggested he 'had not studied composition regularly at an early period of his life; and was but little used to writing in many parts'.[13]

With attitudes of this sort, it is not surprising that the revival of Dowland's music essentially had to wait until the twentieth century. *The First Booke* was edited by William Chappell for The Musical Antiquarian Society in 1844, though complete editions of the voice and lute versions of the songs only appeared in 1922–4, and some of the part-song versions remained unpublished until 1953. The instrumental music had to wait even longer: *Lachrimae* first appeared in 1927, but most of the lute music had to wait until the publication of *CLM* in 1974. Another reason why Dowland's music was neglected so long was that much of it requires the lute and the viol, instruments that were largely out of use between the early eighteenth century and the late nineteenth century. Peter Warlock still assumed modern strings rather than viols in his edition of *Lachrimae* and suggested the independent material in the lute part could be cued into the string parts, or that the part could be played on a harpsichord or even a piano.

Some of the pioneer groups such as the London Consort of Viols and the English Consort of Viols may have performed pieces from *Lachrimae* in the 1930s and 40s, though the first complete recording only appeared in 1957–8. The Elizabethan Players (1957) recorded the seven 'Lachrimae' pavans and ten of the other pieces on viols, but with the treble viols played under the chin, to judge from a photograph in the accompanying leaflet, and a virginals instead of a lute playing only the flourishes at the end of the strains.[14] The first complete recording, by the Philomusica of London directed by Thurston Dart (*c.* 1957–8), uses a modern string orchestra with lute and harpsichord.[15] Six of the seven subsequent complete recordings, by the Schola Cantorum Basiliensis (1962), the Consort of Musicke (1979), the Dowland Consort (1985), Hesperion XX (1987), Fretwork (1989–90) and the Rose Consort (1992, 1997), use the same scoring, a viol consort with lute, though comparisons between them reveal much about changing attitudes to the disposition of instruments, stringing, tuning, vibrato, styles of bowing, articulation and ornamentation. The recording by The Parley of Instruments (1992) uses a Renaissance violin consort with a lute, and transposes the low-pitched pieces up a fourth, as discussed in Chapter 2.[16]

Today, Dowland's music is more popular than at any time in the 400 years since it was written; indeed, *Lachrimae* is probably the most recorded and performed collection of instrumental music before the Water Music or the Brandenburg Concertos. In many ways, Dowland's position in our musical culture invites comparison with that occupied by Elgar, born almost 300 years later. They were both outsiders denied advancement by the English establishment, whose gifts were recognised earlier on the Continent than at home. They were complex and somewhat contradictory personalities, whose acute sense of melancholy and failure prevented them from enjoying fame and fortune, and whose inspiration seems to have deserted them just as they finally achieved the recognition of their compatriots. Dowland's music certainly expresses as powerfully as Elgar's a sense of melancholy and regret, made the more intense for being expressed in conventional musical forms and idioms. In an age of instant fame, relentless fashion and mindless experiment their music speaks to us with a peculiar eloquence.

Notes

1 The document

1 The following account is based on R. Steele, *The Earliest English Music Printing* (London, 1903; repr. 1965); J. Kerman, *The Elizabethan Madrigal: A Comparative Study* (New York, 1962), 258–67; D. W. Krummel, *English Music Printing 1553–1700* (London, 1975); I. Fenlon and J. Milsom, '"Ruled Paper Imprinted": Music Paper and Patents in Sixteenth-Century England', *JAMS* 37 (1984), 139–63.

2 Steele, *The Earliest English Music Printing*, 26–7.

3 E. Arber, *A Transcript of the Registers of the Company of Stationers of London 1554–1640*, III (London, 1876), 94.

4 Steele, *The Earliest English Music Printing*, 27–8.

5 For Dowland's continental career, see *JD*, 30–52; *DM*, 16–19, 99–105.

6 K. Sparr, 'Some Unobserved Information about John Dowland, Thomas Campion and Philip Rosseter', *The Lute* 27 (1987), 35–7.

7 *JD*, 60–1; see also D. Pinto, 'Dowland's Tears: Aspects of *Lachrimae*', *The Lute* 37 (1997), 44–75.

8 *JD*, 274–5; Arber, *A Transcript*, III, 228.

9 Arber, *A Transcript*, III, 258.

10 Krummel, *English Music Printing*, 47–50.

11 *Ibid.*, 88.

12 *Ibid.*, 107, 110; Krummel's account is confused at this point: in fig. 39A he wrongly associates the rhythm shapes used in *Lachrimae* with Short rather than Barley.

13 US-Ws, V.b. 280; manuscript formerly in the possession of Robert Spencer, now in GB-Lam, ff. 12v, 83v; see J. M. Ward, 'The So-Called "Dowland Lute Book" in the Folger Shakespeare Library', *JLSA* 9 (1976), 4–29; *idem*, *Music for Elizabethan Lutes* (Oxford, 1992), I, 52; there are facsimiles in A. Rooley, 'John Dowland and English Lute Music', *EM* 3 (1975), 117; *The Board Lute Book*, ed. R. Spencer (Leeds, 1976).

14 *The First Set of Songs in Four Parts, Composed by John Dowland*, ed. W. Chappell (London, 1844), 2; *Catalogue of the Music Library of Edward Francis Rimbault*, ed. A. Hyatt King (Buren, 1975).

15 M. Dowling, 'The Printing of John Dowland's Second Booke of Ayres', *The Library*, 4th series, 12 (1932), 365–80; see *JD*, 246–7; Kerman, *The Elizabethan Madrigal*, 262–3.

16 Edwards, 1; the date has been removed from the Performers' Facsimile edition of the British Library copy.

17 W. A. Jackson, *Records of the Court of the Stationers' Company, 1602–40* (London, 1957), 19, 39–40.

18 The modern edition, *Canzonets to Five and Six Voices 1597*, ed. E. Fellowes, rev. S. Dunkley, The English Madrigalists 3 (London, 2/1977), does not include the lute part; see Kerman, *The Elizabethan Madrigal*, 165–9.

19 There is a facsimile in *Grove 6*, XVII, 715; see J. Noble, 'Le répertoire instrumental anglais: 1550–1585', *La musique instrumentale de la Renaissance*, ed. J. Jacquot (Paris, 1954), 91–114; W. Edwards, 'The Sources of Elizabethan Consort Music', Ph.D. thesis (University of Cambridge (1974), I, 90–7. Edwards's suggestion that the manuscript is in the hand of Clement Woodcock is rejected in R. Ford, 'Clement Woodcock's Appointment at Canterbury Cathedral', *Chelys* 16 (1987), 36–43.

20 S. F. Pogue, *Jacques Moderne: Lyons Music Printer of the Sixteenth Century* (Geneva, 1969), 74–9; Krummel, *The Earliest Music Printing*, 106.

21 A. Orologio, *Canzonette a tre voci*, ed. F. Colussi, Opera omnia 1 (Udine, 1993).

22 A. Holborne, *Music for Cittern*, ed. M. Kanazawa, Complete Works 2 (Cambridge, Mass., 1973), especially the facsimile on p. 7.

23 'Morley's Consort' and 'Rosseters Consort' are listed among the 'Musick Bookes in folio' in J. Playford, *A Catalogue of all the Musick-Bookes that have been Printed in England, either for Voyce or Instruments* (London, [1653]), reproduced in L. Coral, 'A John Playford Advertisement', *RMARC* 5 (1965), 1–12; see T. Morley, *The First Book of Consort Lessons*, ed. S. Beck (New York, 1959); I. Harwood, 'Rosseter's *Lessons for Consort* of 1609', *LSJ* 7 (1965), 15–23.

24 I am grateful to Ian Harwood for this information.

25 I am grateful to Alison Crum and Richard Rastall for advice on this point.

26 W. Edwards, 'The Performance of Ensemble Music in Elizabethan England', *PRMA* 97 (1970–71), 113–23; see also P. Doe, 'The Emergence of the In Nomine: Some Notes and Queries on the Work of Tudor Church Musicians', *Modern Musical Scholarship*, ed. E. Olleson (Stocksfield, 1978), 79–92; I. Woodfield, *The Early History of the Viol* (Cambridge, 1984),

216–19; R. Rastall, 'Spatial Effects in English Instrumental Consort Music, *c*1560–1605', *EM* 25 (1997), 269–88. David Pinto has recently pointed out that the title of Add. MS 31390 was added several decades after most of the contents, and is therefore of questionable value as evidence of performance practice; see 'Purcell's In Nomines: A Tale of Two Manuscripts (perhaps Three)', *Chelys* 25 (1996/7), 103–4.

27 O. H. Mies, 'Elizabethan Music Prints in an East-Prussian Castle', *MD* 3 (1949), 171–2; one of these copies was subsequently owned by Robert Spencer, see Edwards, 1.

28 A. Holborne, *Pavans, Galliards, Almains 1599*, ed. B. Thomas (London, 1980).

29 The entry 'Dowlands fift Booke' among the 'Musick Bookes in folio' in Playford, *A Catalogue*, is probably a reference to *Lachrimae*.

30 *JD*, 86.

2 The instruments

1 Recent studies of this subject are Woodfield, *The Early History of the Viol*; K. Polk, *German Instrumental Music of the Late Middle Ages* (Cambridge, 1992); *Fiddlers*, ch. 1; Polk, 'Innovation in Instrumental Music 1450–1520: The Role of German Performers within European Culture', *Music in the German Renaissance: Sources, Styles, and Contexts*, ed. J. Kmetz (Cambridge, 1994), 202–14.

2 *Fiddlers*, 58–87.

3 *Ibid.*, 123–7.

4 Edwards, 'The Sources', I, 50; see also *Fiddlers*, 127.

5 *Fiddlers*, 128–9.

6 *Ibid.*, 132–9, contains a survey of the mixed consort and its sources.

7 C. Butler, *The Principles of Musik in Singing and Setting* (London, 1636), 94.

8 A. Gurr, *The Shakespearean Stage 1574–1642* (Cambridge, 1970), 19; J. Limon, *Gentlemen of a Company: English Players in Central and Eastern Europe, 1590–1660* (Cambridge, 1985), 4–6.

9 P. E. Mueller, 'The Influence and Activities of English Musicians on the Continent during the Late Sixteenth and Early Seventeenth Centuries', Ph.D. diss., Indiana University (1954), 2, 9.

10 W. Brade, *Newe außerlesene Paduanen, Galliarden* (Hamburg, 1609), ed. B. Thomas (London, 1982); *idem, Newe außerlesene Paduanen und Galliarden* (Hamburg, 1614), ed. Thomas (London, 1992); T. Simpson, *Opusculum neuwer Pavanen* (Frankfurt, 1610), ed. H. Mönkemeyer (Celle, 1987); *idem, Opus newer Paduanen* (Hamburg, 1617), ed. Thomas (London, 1997); *idem, Taffel-Consort* (Hamburg, 1621), ed. Thomas (London, 1988).

11   *Außerlesener Paduanen und Galliarden Erster Theil* (Hamburg, 1607), ed. H. Mönkemeyer (Celle, 1986); *Ander Theil Außerlesener lieblicher Paduanen* (Hamburg, 1609), ed. Mönkemeyer (Celle, 1986); W. Brade, *Newe Außerlesene liebliche Branden* (Hamburg and Lübeck, 1617), ed. B. Thomas (London, 1974); E. H. Meyer, *Die mehrstimmige Spielmusik des 17. Jahrhunderts in Nord- und Mitteleuropa* (Kassel, 1934), 235.

12   M. Praetorius, *Syntagma musicum II: De Organographia Parts I and II*, ed. D. Z. Crookes (Oxford, 1986), 52; see also *Fiddlers*, 19, 168.

13   M. Riley, 'The Teaching of Bowed Instruments from 1511 to 1756', Ph.D. diss., University of Michigan (1954); Woodfield, *The Early History of the Viol*, 104–17, 140–54, 199–201; *Fiddlers*, 21–7.

14   B. Lee, 'Giovanni Maria Lanfranco's *Scintille di musica* and its Relation to Sixteenth-Century Music Theory', Ph.D. diss., Cornell University (1961), 252–3, 259–60.

15   See D. Boyden, 'The Tenor Violin: Myth, Mystery, or Misnomer?' in W. Gerstenberg, J. La Rue and W. Rehm, eds., *Festschrift Otto Erich Deutsch* (Kassel, 1963), 273–9; for Zacconi, see *idem*, 'Monteverdi's *Violini Piccoli alla Francese* and *Viole da Brazzo*', *Annales musicologiques* 6 (1958–63), 393; *idem*, *The History of Violin Playing from its Origins to 1761* (London, 1965), 42–3; for Hitzler, see Riley, 'The Teaching of Bowed Instruments', 239–41; E. Segerman, 'Hizler's [*sic*] Tenor Violin', *FoMRHIQ* 27 (April 1982), 38.

16   Praetorius, *Syntagma musicum*, ed. Crookes, 39.

17   Mersenne, *Harmonie universelle: The Books on Instruments*, trans. R. E. Chapman (The Hague, 1957), 238, 244.

18   H. L. Hassler, *Lustgarten neuer teutscher Gesäng (1601)*, ed. C. R. Crosby, Sämliche Werke 9 (Wiesbaden, 1968).

19   A. Orologio, *Intradae Quinque et Sex Vocibus Liber Primus*, ed. G. Perisan, Opera omnia 7 (Udine, 1995).

20   C. Wool, 'A Critical Edition and Historical Commentary of Kassel 4° MS Mus. 125', M. Mus. diss., London (1983); *Moritz Landgraf of Hessen, The Kassel Pavan Collection: I*, ed. B. Thomas (London, 1994); see *Fiddlers*, 157–63.

21   *Eight Short Elizabethan Dance Tunes*, ed. P. Warlock (London, 1924); C. Monson, *Voices and Viols in England, 1600–1650: The Sources and the Music* (Ann Arbor, Mich., 1982), 159–79.

22   For *chiavette* and the transposition of instrumental music, see P. Barbieri, '*Chiavette* and Modal Transposition in Italian Practice (*c.* 1500–1837)', *Recercare* 3 (1991), 5–79; P. Van Heyghen, 'The Recorder in Italian Music, 1600–1700', *The Recorder in the Seventeenth Century: Proceedings of the International Recorder Symposium, Utrecht 1993*, ed. D. Lasocki (Utrecht, 1995), 3–63, especially 24–6, 58.

23 See especially D. Abbott and E. Segerman, 'Strings in the Sixteenth and Seventeenth Centuries', *GSJ* 27 (1974), 48–73; S. Bonta, 'Further Thoughts on the History of Strings', *The Catgut Acoustical Society Newsletter* 26 (November 1976), 21–6; *idem*, 'From Violone to Violoncello: A Question of Strings?' *JAMIS* 3 (1977), 64–99; *idem*, 'Catline Strings Revisited', *JAMIS* 14 (1988), 38–60; M. Peruffo, 'New Hypothesis on the Construction of Bass Strings for Lutes and other Gut-Strung Instruments', *FoMRHIQ* 62 (January 1991), 22–36; *idem*, 'On Venice Catlins, Lyons, Pistoy-Basses and Loaded-Weighted Bass Gut Strings', *FoMRHIQ* 76 (July 1994), 72–84; Segerman, 'Gut Stringing for Lutes', *Lute News* 45 (March 1998), 13–18.

24 Praetorius, *Syntagma musicum*, ed. Crookes, 52–3.

25 The most recent and authoritative study is B. Haynes, 'Pitch Standards in the Baroque and Classical Period', Ph.D. thesis, Université de Montréal (1995).

26 I. Harwood, 'A Case of Double Standards? Instrumental Pitch in England *c.* 1600', *EM* 9 (1981), 470–81.

27 Ed. P. Doe, MB 44 (London, 1979), nos. 48–50.

28 W. Byrd, *Keyboard Music: II*, MB 28 (London, 2/1976), no. 54; J. P. Sweelinck, *Keyboard Works (Settings of Secular Tunes and Dances)*, ed. F. Noske, Opera omnia – Editio altera 3 (Amsterdam, 2/1974), no. 10; GB-Lbl, Add. MSS 17786–91, f. 14; GB-Eu, La.III.483, pp. 184, 202; GB-Lbl, Add. MS 33933, f. 86; Morley, *Consort Lessons*, ed. Beck, no. 7; see *Fiddlers*, 136–8, for arguments that the top parts of mixed consorts were primarily intended for the violin rather than the treble viol.

29 O. Vecchi, *Arie, Canzonette e Balli*, ed. O. Chilesotti (Milan, 1892; repr. 1968), 34–8.

30 W. Salmen, *Musikleben im 16. Jahrhundert*, Musikgeschichte in Bildern III/9 (Leipzig, 1976), 161; *Fiddlers*, 117 and pl. 3b.

31 For lute stringing and tuning, see D. Poulton, 'Lute Stringing in the Light of the Surviving Tablatures', *LSJ* 6 (1964), 14–24; *JD*, 341, 456–7; Ward, *Music for Elizabethan Lutes*, I, 25–8.

32 F. Caroso, *Nobiltà di dame*, ed. J. Sutton and F. M. Walker (Oxford, 1986).

33 The viol parts mentioned on the title-page do not seem to survive, and may never have been published.

34 P. Holman, '"Evenly, Softly, and Sweetly Acchording to All": The Organ Accompaniment of English Consort Music', *John Jenkins and his Time: Studies in English Consort Music*, ed. A. Ashbee and Holman (Oxford, 1996), 353–82; L. U. Mortensen, '"Unerringly Tasteful"?: Harpsichord Continuo in Corelli's op. 5 Sonatas', *EM* 24 (1996), 665–79.

35 Edited in Morley, *Consort Lessons*, ed. Beck, no. 6.
36 Harwood, 'A Case of Double Standards', 477–8.

3 The dance types

1 J. Ward, 'The Maner of Dauncying', *EM* 4 (1976), 139, 142; see also *Calendar of Letters, Despatches, and State Papers, Relating to the Negotiations between England and Spain, Preserved at the Archives at Simancas and Elsewhere* 2, ed. G. A. Bergenroth (London, 1866), 445.

2 T. Arbeau, *Orchesography*, trans. C. W. Beaumont (London, 1925); see also B. Thomas and J. Gingell, *The Renaissance Dance Book* (London, 1987).

3 T. Morley, *A Plain and Easy Introduction to Practical Music*, ed. R. A. Harman (London, 2/1963), 296–7.

4 R. Hudson, *The Allemande, the Balletto, and the Tanz* (Cambridge, 1986).

5 See, for instance, Thomas and Gingell, *The Renaissance Dance Book*, 108–14; *Italian Dances of the Early Sixteenth Century*, ed. M. Morrow, Dance Music of the Middle Ages and Renaissance 1 (London, 1976).

6 See J. Ward, 'And Who but Ladie Greensleeves', *The Well Enchanting Skill: Essays in Honour of Frederick W. Sternfeld*, ed. J. Caldwell, E. Olleson and S. Wollenberg (Oxford, 1990), 181–211.

7 Arbeau, *Orchesography*, 58–9; Hudson, *The Allemande, the Balletto, and the Tanz*; W. Byrd, *Keyboard Music: I*, ed. A. Brown, MB 27 (London, 2/1976), no. 21a; Morley, *Consort Lessons*, ed. Beck, no. 22.

8 *The Fitzwilliam Virginal Book*, ed. J. A. Fuller Maitland and W. Barclay Squire (London and Leipzig, 1894–9; repr. 1963), no. 85; see also, P. Dirksen, *The Keyboard Music of Jan Pieterzoon Sweelinck* (Utrecht, 1997), 297–308; *Fiddlers*, 144–6.

9 GB-Lbl, Royal Appendix MSS 74–6; complete edition in *Elizabethan Consort Music: I*, ed. P. Doe, MB 44 (London, 1979), nos. 76–111, App. 1–22; see *Fiddlers*, 90–103.

10 H. M. Brown, *Embellishing Sixteenth-Century Music* (London, 1976) is a useful introduction to the subject.

11 See A. Rooley and J. Tyler, 'The Lute Consort', *LSJ* 14 (1972), 13–24; there is a selection from the Holmes manuscripts in *Music for Mixed Consort*, ed. W. Edwards, MB 40 (London, 1977), nos. 16–27.

12 *Tudor Keyboard Music c1520–1580*, ed. J. Caldwell, MB 66 (London, 1995), nos. 39–44; reconstructed four-part consort versions are in *Seven Dances from the Court of Henry VIII*, ed. P. Holman (Corby, 1983); see *Fiddlers*, 68–9.

13 J. d'Estrée, *Premier Livre de Danseries 1559*, ed. B. Thomas (London, 1991); C. Cunningham, 'Estienne du Tertre, scavant Musicien, Jean d'Estrée,

joueur de hautbois du Roy, and the Mid-Sixteenth Century Franco-Flemish Chanson and Ensemble Dance', Ph.D. diss., Bryn Mawr College (1969).

14 *London, British Library MS Egerton 3665 ('The Tregian Manuscript')*, ed. F. A. D'Accone, Renaissance Music in Facsimile 7 (New York, 1988), II, ff. 514–523; see *Fiddlers*, 148–55.

15 W. Byrd, *My Ladye Nevells Booke of Virginal Music*, ed. H. Andrews (London, 1926; repr. 1969), nos. 10–21, 24–5, 39–40; I. Harwood, 'Rosseter's *Lessons for Consort* of 1609', *LSJ* 7 (1965), 15–23.

16 See *Fiddlers*, 164–8.

17 *Ibid.*, 145–8.

18 A point made by Bernard Thomas in Simpson, *Taffel-Consort*, iv.

19 *Elizabethan Consort Music: I*, ed. Doe, no. 101; the attribution to Innocent comes from the Quintus of the galliard, which Doe prints separately as App. 3.

20 *The Dublin Virginal Book*, ed. J. M. Ward (London, 1983), no. 5; Kerman, *The Elizabethan Madrigal*, 91–2; *Fiddlers*, 151–2.

21 *Music for Mixed Consort*, ed. Edwards, no. 30; Wool, 'A Critical Edition', II, no. 34.

22 *Elizabethan Consort Music: I*, ed. Doe, nos. 83–5, 106.

23 For example, *ibid.*, no. 109; *The Dublin Virginal Book*, ed. Ward, no. 3; *Tisdale's Virginal Book*, ed. A. Brown (London, 1966), no. 6.

24 A. Bassano, *Pavans and Galliards in Five Parts*, ed. P. Holman (London, 1981), no. 1.

25 Morley, *Consort Lessons*, ed. Beck, no. 13; Wool, 'A Critical Edition', II, no. 20.

26 *Music for Mixed Consort*, ed. Edwards, no. 29; Wool, 'A Critical Edition', II, nos. 4, 35, 36, 40 and 48.

27 *The Tregian Manuscript*, ed. D'Accone, ff. 517v–519; T. Tomkins, *Consort Music*, ed. J. Irving, MB 59, no. 26; see *Fiddlers*, 150–1.

28 Morley, *A Plain and Easy Introduction*, ed. Harman, 249.

29 *The Works of Thomas Campion*, ed. W. R. Davis (London, 1969), 319–56.

30 A-Wn, MS 17771, f. 221v; see G. Hendrie, 'The Keyboard Music of Orlando Gibbons', *PRMA* 89 (1962–3), 1–15; H. Ferguson, *Keyboard Interpretation* (London, 1975), 105–9; D. Wulstan, *Tudor Music* (London, 1985), 118–20.

31 *The Principles of Musik*, 83.

32 *Elizabethan Consort Music: 1*, ed. Doe, no. 82.

4 The seven 'Passionate Pavans'

1 See the lists in *JD*, 487–8, 500–1, 505–6; *DM*, 60–1, 75–6, 80; Dirksen, *Sweelinck*, 308.

2 *CLM*, no. 15; for Holmes, see I. Harwood, 'The Origins of the Cambridge Lute Manuscripts', *LSJ* 5 (1963), 32–48. Robert Spencer suggested to me that the version in the Board Manuscript, ff. 11v–12, was corrected by Dowland himself; see the facsimile edition, ed. Spencer.

3 *JD*, 126; R. Spencer, 'Dowland's Dance Songs: Those of his Compositions which Exist in Two Versions, Songs and Instrumental Dances', *Concert des voix et des instruments à la renaissance: Actes du colloque organisé en 1991 par Le Centre d'Etudes Supérieures de la Renaissance, Université François-Rabelais, Tours* (Paris, 1995), 587–99; see also E. Doughtie, *English Renaissance Song* (Boston, 1986), 128.

4 *JD*, 126–7.

5 *Fiddlers*, 160.

6 This discussion is indebted to L. Pike, *Expression and the Evolution of Musical Language* (forthcoming), ch. 6.

7 G. Zarlino, *On the Modes: Part Four of 'Le istitutioni harmoniche', 1558*, trans. V. Cohen, ed. C. Palisca (New Haven and London, 1983), 81–3.

8 O. Mies, 'Dowland's Lachrimae Tune', *MD* 4 (1950), 59–64; *JD*, 125–6.

9 R. Henning, 'A Possible Source of Lachrimae', *LSJ* 16 (1974), 65–7.

10 *DM*, 61, 82.

11 Pike, *Expression and the Evolution of Musical Language*; E. Rosand, 'The Descending Tetrachord: An Emblem of Lament', *MQ* 65 (1979), 346–59.

12 *CLM*, nos. 2, 3; see D. Hofmann, 'The Chromatic Fourth', *The Consort* 26 (1970), 445–58; P. Williams, *The Chromatic Fourth during Four Centuries of Music* (Oxford, 1997), 7–37.

13 Pinto, 'Dowland's Tears'; O. Lassus, *The Seven Penitential Psalms and Laudate Domine de caelis*, ed. P. Berquist (Madison, Wisc., 1990), 10–11.

14 *Luca Marenzio Opera Omnia V*, ed. B. Meier, CMM 72 ([Stuttgart], 1983), 26–31; A. Obertello, *Madrigali italiani in Inghilterra* (Milan, 1949), 135–6, a reference brought to my attention by David Pinto.

15 A. Rooley, 'New Light on John Dowland's Songs of Darkness', *EM* 11 (1983), 6–21.

16 A. Newcomb, *The Madrigal at Ferrara 1579–1597* (Princeton, 1980), II, 170–7.

17 Kerman, *The Elizabethan Madrigal*, 40–72; Morley, *A Plain and Easy Introduction*, ed. Harman, 294.

18 Morley, *A Plain and Easy Introduction*, ed. Harman, 290–1.

19 R. H. Wells, *Elizabethan Mythologies: Studies in Poetry, Drama and Music* (Cambridge, 1994), 86–8.

20 R. Toft, *Tune thy Musicke to thy Hart: The Art of Eloquent Singing in England 1597–1622* (Toronto, 1993), 4.

21 In particular, R. Spencer, 'Performance Style of the English Lute Ayre
    c. 1600', *The Lute* 24 (1984), 55–68; R. Toft, *Tune thy Musicke to thy Hart*;
    S. M. Pauly, 'Rhetoric and the Performance of Seventeenth-Century
    English Continuo Song', D.M.A. diss., Stanford University (1995).

22 Toft, *Tune thy Musicke to thy Hart*, 26–41; see also W. Taylor, *Tudor Figures
    of Rhetoric* (Whitewater, Wisc., 1972), 78–9; D. Bartel, *Musica poetica:
    Musical-Rhetorical Figures in German Baroque Music* (Lincoln, Nebr., and
    London, 1997), 179–80, 220–4.

23 Toft, *Tune thy Musicke to thy Hart*, 33–4.

24 *Ibid.*, 82; Bartel, *Musica poetica*, 180.

25 Toft, *Tune thy Musicke to thy Hart*, 43; see also Taylor, *Tudor Figures of Rhet-
    oric*, 117–18.

26 Toft, *Tune thy Musicke to thy Hart*, 46.

27 Simpson, *Opusculum neuwer Pavanen*, ed. Mönkemeyer, no. 3.

28 R. Rastall, *The Heaven Singing: Music in Early English Religious Drama*, I
    (Cambridge, 1996), 234; Pinto, 'Dowland's Tears'; Pike, *Expression and the
    Evolution of Musical Language*.

29 Kerman, *The Elizabethan Madrigal*, 6–7.

30 C. Tye, *English Sacred Music*, ed. J. Morehen, EECM 19 (London, 1977),
    99–124; T. Morley, *English Anthems, Liturgical Music*, ed. J. Morehen,
    EECM 38 (London, 1991), 11–23; T. Weelkes, *Collected Anthems*, ed. D.
    Brown, W. Collins and P. Le Huray, MB 23 (London, 2/1975), no. 18; see P.
    Le Huray, *Music and the Reformation in England 1549–1660* (London, 1967),
    204, 251, 304–5.

31 Edited in *Jacobean Consort Music*, ed. T. Dart and W. Coates, MB 9
    (London, 2/1966), nos. 62, 63.

32 M. E. Lange, *Telling Tears in the English Renaissance*, Studies in the History
    of Christian Thought 70 (Leiden, New York, Cologne, 1996), 39.

33 J. Donne, *The Divine Poems*, ed. H. Gardner (Oxford, 2/1978), 13.

34 Lange, *Telling Tears*, 129–47.

35 P. Warlock, *The English Ayre* (London, 1926), 39; E. H. Meyer, *Early English
    Chamber Music* (London, 2/1982), 131–3; *JD*, 342–56; Edwards, 2.

36 Rooley, 'New Light', 19; R. H. Wells, 'John Dowland and Elizabethan
    Melancholy', *EM* 13 (1985), 514–28, revised as 'Dowland, Ficino and Eliza-
    bethan Melancholy', *Elizabethan Mythologies*, 189–207.

37 'Dowland's Tears' and personal communication.

38 *St. Augustine's Confessions with an English Translation by William Watts 1631*, ed.
    W. H. D. Rouse (Cambridge, Mass., and London, 1912; repr. 1977), II, 146–7.

39 *JD*, 28; Library of Hatfield House, C. P. 173, ff. 91–92ᵛ, there is a moder-
    nised transcription in *JD*, 37–40.

40 R. Burton, *The Anatomy of Melancholy*, ed. T. C. Faulkner, N. K. Kiessling and R. L. Blair (Oxford, 1989–94).

41 L. Babb, *The Elizabethan Malady: A Study of Melancholia in English Literature from 1580 to 1642* (East Lansing, Mich., 1951), 184–5.

42 Burton, *The Anatomy of Melancholy*, ed. Faulkner, Kiessling and Blair, I, 74–5.

43 See in particular, Babb, *The Elizabethan Malady*, 1–72.

44 GB-Lbl, Add. MS 27579, f. 88; see *JD*, 60, 399 and illus. 6b.

45 *JD*, 215, 343.

46 L. A. Austern, 'Nature, Culture, Myth and the Musician in Early Modern England', *JAMS* 51 (1998), 36.

47 Burton, *The Anatomy of Melancholy*, ed. Faulkner, Kiessling and Blair, II, 112–14, 116.

48 Toft, *Tune the Musicke to thy Hart*, 21, 44; Bartel, *Musica Poetica*, 334–9.

49 D. Leech-Wilkinson, 'My Lady's Tears: A Pair of Songs by John Dowland', *EM* 19 (1991), 227–33; see also the reply by David Pinto, 'Dowland's Lachrymal Airs', *EM* 20 (1992), 525.

50 Burton, *The Anatomy of Melancholy*, ed. Faulkner, Kiessling and Blair, III, 330–445.

51 *Ibid.*, III, 197, 413–14.

52 Babb, *The Elizabethan Malady*, 73–101.

53 *Ibid.*, 80.

54 A point made in Pike, *Expression and the Evolution of Musical Language*.

55 Bartel, *Musica poetica*, 394–7.

56 Burton, *The Anatomy of Melancholy*, ed. Faulkner, Kiessling and Blair, I, 400.

57 Babb, *The Elizabethan Malady*, 64.

58 Burton, *The Anatomy of Melancholy*, ed. Faulkner, Kiessling and Blair, III, 29.

59 Babb, *The Elizabethan Malady*, 178–80: J. Milton, *Poetical Works*, II, ed. H. Darbishire (Oxford, 1955), 142–6.

60 *JD*, 355–6, relates the passage to bb. 13–14 of 'I saw my Lady weepe', but the relevant chord there is 6♮–3♯ rather than 6♭–3♯.

5 'Divers other Pavans, Galiards, and Almands'

1 *Il nuovo Vogel: Bibliografia della musica italiana vocale profana*, ed. F. Lesure and C. Sartori (Geneva, 1977–83), 999–1035.

2 R. Tatlow, *Bach and the Riddle of the Number Alphabet* (Cambridge, 1991), especially 33; I owe this idea to Tim Carter.

3 J. H. Schein, *Banchetto musicale 1617*, ed. B. Thomas (London, 1993).

4 Wool, 'A Critical Edition', II, no. 49.

5　A point made in Pinto, 'Dowland's Tears'.

6　Edwards, 2.

7　*The Diary of John Manningham*, ed. R. P. Sorlien (Hanover, NH, 1976), 150; *JD*, 119–20; *St Augustine's Confessions with an English Translation by William Watts 1631*, I, 40–1.

8　Toft, *Tune thy Musicke to thy Hart*, 47–8, 167.

9　*CLM*, no. 9; *JD*, 120.

10　GB-Ge, R.d.43, f. 25; MS in the possession of Lord Forester, f. 14v; I am grateful to Matthew Spring for advice on this point.

11　For Unton, see R. Strong, 'Sir Henry Unton and his Portrait: An Elizabethan Memorial Picture and its History', *Archaeologia* 99 (1965), 53–76; *JD*, 431–3; A. Rooley, 'A Portrait of Sir Henry Unton', *Companion to Mediaeval and Renaissance Music*, ed. T. Knighton and D. Fallows (Oxford, 2/1997), 85–92.

12　Edwards, 3; A. Holborne, *Music for Lute and Bandora*, The Complete Works 1 (Cambridge, Mass., 1967), no. 13.

13　*JD*, 414.

14　G. Zarlino, *On the Modes*, trans. Cohen, ed. Palisca, 67, 85.

15　*CLM*, nos. 14, 14a.

16　Notes to P. O'Dette, *John Dowland: Complete Lute Works* 3, Harmonia Mundi HMU 907162; see, for instance, *CLM*, nos. 5, 17, 18.

17　*JD*, 359.

18　*CLM*, nos. 23, 95.

19　*Ibid.*, no. 42; see Spencer, 'Dowland's Dance-Songs', 595–9.

20　Doughtie, *English Renaissance Song*, 129–31; see also *JD*, 226–30.

21　*DM*, 73–4.

22　D. Poulton, 'Captain Digory Piper of the Sweepstake', *LSJ* 4 (1962), 17–22; *JD*, 423–5; *DM*, 60.

23　*CLM*, no. 19.

24　*Ibid.*, no. 34.

25　E. B. Jorgens, *The Well-Tun'd Word: Musical Interpretations of English Poetry 1597–1651* (Minneapolis, 1982), 150–1; see also *JD*, 296–7.

26　Arbeau, *Orchesography*, ed. Beaumont, 94; see *JD*, 149.

27　*JD*, 421–2.

28　*Ibid.*, 145–6, 223–4; *DM*, 63–4.

29　*CLM*, no. 26; *JD*, 429.

30　*DM*, 64–5, 82–4; see also Edwards, 3.

31　Byrd, *Keyboard Music: II*, ed. Brown, nos. 54, 55; GB-Lbl, Add. MSS 17786–91, nos. 30, 31; *Eight Short Elizabethan Dances*, ed. Fellowes, no. 1; see, for instance, 'Galliard Can she excuse and may serve to Lacrimae', *Tisdale's Virginal Book*, ed. Brown, no. 7; *CLM*, no. 46.

32 *CLM*, no. 29.

33 *French Chansons of the Sixteenth Century*, ed. J. A. Bernstein (University Park, Penn., and London, 1985), no. 26; *CLM*, no. 91; *Erster Theil*, ed. Mönkemeyer, 41; *CLM*, no. 38; see also *DM*, 28–9.

34 *Fiddlers*, 151.

35 *DM*, 81.

36 *JD*, 138–42; *DM*, 61–2; Byrd, *Keyboard Music: II*, ed. Brown, no. 94; J. Bull, *Keyboard Music: II*, ed. T. Dart, MB 19 (London, 1970), no. 108.

37 *CLM*, nos. 33, 20, 39.

38 *The Principles of Musik*, 2.

39 *CLM*, no. 40.

40 *Mr William Shakespeare's Comedies, Histories, & Tragedies* (1623; repr. 1954); see also C. Dollerup, *Denmark, Hamlet and Shakespeare: A Study of Englishmen's Knowledge of Denmark towards the End of the Sixteenth Century with Special Reference to Hamlet* (Salzburg, 1975), 122–7.

41 *JD*, 408.

42 *CLM*, no. 52; V. Haussmann, *Ausgewählte Instrumentalwerke*, ed. F. Boelsche, DDT, series 1, 16 (Leipzig, 1904), 133.

43 *JD*, 371; R. M. Wilson, *Anglican Chant and Chanting in England, Scotland and America 1660–1820* (Oxford, 1996), especially ch. 3.

44 *JD*, 435–6.

6 Reception

1 Simpson, *Opusculum*, ed. Mönkemeyer, 7–8, 32–5; *Fiddlers*, 253–5.

2 Simpson, *Opusculum*, ed. Mönkemeyer, 16–17; *CCM*, nos. 25, 26, 24, 27.

3 For sources, see *JD*, 488; *DM*, 60–1; Dirksen, *Sweelinck*, 308; Sweelinck, *Keyboard Works*, ed. Noske, no. 10; *Lied- und Tanzvariationen der Sweelinck-Schule*, ed. W. Breig (Mainz, 1970), nos. 6, 7.

4 Dirksen, *Sweelinck*, 31–2, 651–2; *Lied- und Tanzvariationen*, ed. Breig, no. 4; S. Scheidt, *Unedierte Kompositionen für Tasteninstrumente*, ed. C. Mahrenholz, Werke 5 (Hamburg, 1957), 31–4.

5 S. Scheidt, *Ludi musici prima pars (1621)*, ed. B. Thomas (London, 1996), 36–9.

6 T. Weelkes, *Five-Part Pavans*, ed. G. Hunter (Urbana, Ill., 1985), no. 2; *Cambridge Consorts: Pavans and Galliards in Five Parts*, ed. I. Payne (St Albans, 1991), no. 19; Tomkins, *Consort Music*, ed. Irving, no. 29; *Außerlesener, Paduanen und Galliarden Erster Theil*, ed. Mönkemeyer, 6–7; Brade, *Pavans and Galliards (1614)*, ed. Thomas, 1–2; Simpson, *Opusculum neuwer Paduanen*, ed. Mönkemeyer, 28–31; Schein, *Banchetto musicale*, ed. Thomas, 28–9, 107.

7 T. Morley, *Keyboard Works*, ed. T. Dart (London, 1959), nos. 5, 6; O. Gibbons, *Keyboard Music*, ed. G. Hendrie, MB 20 (London, 1962), nos. 17, 18, 16.

8 W. Lawes, *The Royall Consort (Old Consort)*, ed. D. Pinto (London, 1995), 104–5; *idem, Consort Sets in Five and Six Parts*, ed. Pinto (London, 1979), 30–2; *idem, Fantasia Suites*, ed. Pinto, MB 60 (London, 1991), no. 15a; J. Jenkins, *Consort Music of Four Parts*, ed. A. Ashbee, MB 26 (London, 1969), no. 57; J. Schop, *Paduanen, Allmanden sowie eine Galliarde und eine Canzone zu 4 Stimmen*, ed. D. Hagge (Zurich, 1982), 23–5.

9 *'t Uitnement Kabinet* VIII, ed. R. Rasch (Amsterdam, 1978), 21–8.

10 T. Crawford, '"L'Amant malheureux": S. L. Weiss and French Music', paper read to the 1995 Royal Musical Association conference.

11 R. van Baak Griffioen, *Jacob van Eyck's Der fluyten lust-hof* (Utrecht, 1991), 75, 138–40, 149–52, 179–81, 249–53; for Joseph Butler, see *Dutch Keyboard Music of the 16th and 17th Centuries*, ed. A. Curtis, Monumenta musica Neerlandica 3 (Amsterdam, 1961), xvii–xix.

12 Baak Griffioen, *Der fluyten lust-hof*, 179–81; see also, *JD*, 490–1; *DM*, 67–8.

13 J. Hawkins, *A General History of the Science and Practice of Music* (London, 1853; repr. 1963), 481–3; C. Burney, *A General History of Music*, ed. F. Mercer (London, 1935; repr. 1957), II, 117.

14 Pye CCL 30121; *The World's Encyclopaedia of Recorded Music*, ed. F. F. Clough and G. J. Cuming, I (Colwyn Bay, 1950), lists an undated recording of 'Langton', 'Denmark', 'Collier', 'Essex', 'Noel', 'Whitehead' and 'Nichol' by a New York string orchestra directed by Max Goberman on the General label.

15 L'Oiseau Lyre OL50163 / OLS164.

16 Harmonia Mundi HM30623; L'Oiseau Lyre Florilegium, DSLO 517, reissued on CD in *John Dowland: The Collected Works*, L'Oiseau Lyre 452 563–2; BIS CD 315; Auvidis Fontalis ES 8701; Virgin VC5 45005; Amon Ra CD-SAR55; Naxos 8.553326; Hyperion CDA66639.

Select bibliography

For editions of music, see the Preface and Abbreviations

Arbeau, T. *Orchesography*, trans. C. W. Beaumont (London, 1925)

Arber, E. *A Transcript of the Registers of the Company of Stationers of London 1554–1640*, III (London, 1876)

Baak Griffioen, R. van *Jacob van Eyck's Der fluyten lust-hof* (Utrecht, 1991)

Babb, L. *The Elizabethan Malady: A Study of Melancholia in English Literature from 1580 to 1642* (East Lansing, Mich., 1951)

Bartel, D. *Musica poetica: Musical-Rhetorical Figures in German Baroque Music* (Lincoln, Nebr., and London, 1997)

Burton, R. *The Anatomy of Melancholy*, ed. T. C. Faulkner, N. K. Kiessling and R. L. Blair (Oxford, 1989–94)

Butler, C. *The Principles of Musik* (London, 1636)

Dirksen, P. *The Keyboard Music of Jan Pieterzoon Sweelinck* (Utrecht, 1997)

Doughtie, E. *English Renaissance Song* (Boston, 1986)

Dowling, M. 'The Printing of John Dowland's Second Booke of Ayres', *The Library*, 4th series, 12 (1932), 365–80

Edwards, W. 'The Sources of Elizabethan Consort Music', Ph.D. thesis, University of Cambridge (1974)

Harwood, I. 'A Case of Double Standards? Instrumental Pitch in England c. 1600', *EM* 9 (1981), 470–81

Holman, P. *Four and Twenty Fiddlers: The Violin at the English Court 1540–1690* (Oxford, 1993; 2/1995)

Kerman, J. *The Elizabethan Madrigal: A Comparative Study* (New York, 1962)

Krummel, D. W. *English Music Printing 1553–1700* (London, 1975)

Lange, M. E. *Telling Tears in the English Renaissance*, Studies in the History of Christian Thought 70 (Leiden, New York, Cologne, 1996)

Leech-Wilkinson, D. 'My Lady's Tears: A Pair of Songs by John Dowland', *EM* 19 (1991), 227–33

Morley, T. *A Plain and Easy Introduction to Practical Music*, ed. R. A. Harman (London, 1952; 2/1963)

Pike, L. *Expression and the Evolution of Musical Language* (forthcoming)

Pinto, D. 'Dowland's Tears: Aspects of *Lachrimae*', *The Lute* 37 (1997), 44–75

Poulton, D. *John Dowland* (London, 1972; 2/1982)

Rooley, A. 'New Light on John Dowland's Songs of Darkness', *EM* 11 (1983), 6–21

Spencer, R. 'Dowland's Dance Songs: Those of his Compositions which Exist in Two Versions, Songs and Instrumental Dances', *Concert des voix et des instruments à la renaissance: Actes du colloque organisé en 1991 par Le Centre d'Etudes Supérieures de la Renaissance, Université François-Rabelais, Tours* (Paris, 1995), 587–99

Taylor, W. *Tudor Figures of Rhetoric* (Whitewater, Wisc., 1972)

Toft, R. *Tune thy Musicke to thy Hart: The Art of Eloquent Singing in England 1597–1622* (Toronto, 1993)

Ward, J. M. *A Dowland Miscellany*, *JLSA* 10 (1977)

Music for Elizabethan Lutes (Oxford, 1992)

Wells, R. H. *Elizabethan Mythologies: Studies in Poetry, Drama and Music* (Cambridge, 1994)

Woodfield, I. *The Early History of the Viol* (Cambridge, 1984)

Wool, C. 'A Critical Edition and Historical Commentary of Kassel 4° MS Mus. 125', M. Mus. diss., University of London (1983)

Zarlino, G. *On the Modes: Part Four of 'Le istitutioni harmoniche', 1558*, trans. V. Cohen, ed. C. Palisca (New Haven and London, 1983)

Index